FERNS OF MINNESOTA

FERNS
of
MINNESOTA

Second edition, revised

ROLLA TRYON

Illustrated by Wilma Monserud

University of Minnesota Press

Minneapolis

Copyright © 1954, 1980 by the University of Minnesota
All rights reserved
Published by the University of Minnesota Press
2037 University Avenue Southeast
Minneapolis, Minnesota 55414
2nd edition, revised of
The Ferns and Fern Allies of Minnesota

Library of Congress Cataloging in Publication Data

Tryon, Rolla Milton, 1916-
 Ferns of Minnesota.
  Edition for 1954 published under title: The ferns
and fern allies of Minnesota.
  Bibliography: p.
  Includes index.
  1. Ferns—Minnesota—Identification. 2. Pterido-
phyta—Minnesota—Identification. I. Title.
[QK525.5.M6T7 1980]   587'.309776   80-10368
ISBN 0-8166-0932-2
ISBN 0-8166-0935-7 pbk.

Preface

The period of some 25 years that has elapsed since the publication of Dr. Rolla Tryon's guide to the identification of the ferns and fern allies of Minnesota has been one of sustained interest in these plants on the part of students and the general public alike. Also, the modern emphasis on the need for preservation of natural areas has placed a premium on easily usable and accurate guides to identification of these and other groups of plants. In view of these factors, the Botany Department was pleased to learn some three or four years ago of Dr. Tryon's willingness to prepare a new edition of his Guide. In the new edition he has introduced essential name changes and comments to bring the text into harmony with more recent investigations. At the same time he has left intact the largely nontechnical approach most valued by the nonspecialist. Comments on hybrids appear at the end of the discussion of the respective genera where they occur. The section on ferns in the garden has been completely rewritten, and the inclusion of photographs of species in their natural habitats provides an additional focus of interest to the reader. The greatly extended knowledge of fern distributions in the state is reflected in the more detailed maps. Collectively, these changes represent substantial improvements over the earlier edition and should increase the pleasure in the study of ferns and fern allies afforded to the public to which this volume is addressed. Dr. Tryon has provided a useful and lasting service to the residents of the state of Minnesota.

Gerald B. Ownbey
Curator of the Herbarium
University of Minnesota

Contents

FERNS OF MINNESOTA

Introduction

Ferns are a conspicuous part of the vegetation in Minnesota except in the prairie region. There they are few both in species and in numbers, as would be expected of a group that thrives best in a cool, moist climate and mostly in shaded places. In many suitable areas, especially in the northeastern and southeastern parts of the state, the ferns are the most abundant plants of the ground cover. This book is intended as a guide to the identification of the kinds of ferns, supplying at the same time information on the habitat preferences of the species and their distribution. Ferns lack the showy flowers so common in the seed plants, but their varied and beautiful or unusual leaves have made them a favored group for study by people interested in plant life.

GEOGRAPHY

The total precipitation in Minnesota varies from about 20 inches a year in the northwestern corner of the state to about 32 inches in the southeastern corner. The northwestern corner also has the shortest growing season, about 105 days; the southeastern corner has the longest, about 145 days.

The western edge of the state and the southwestern and southern parts were originally prairie areas; the rest of the state was wooded with either hardwoods or conifers. The hardwood forests occurred in the counties adjacent to the Mississippi River, west to McLeod and north to Pine counties and then generally west and north through Todd and Otter Tail counties to Red Lake and the eastern portion of Kittson County. South and west of this woods was the prairie, and north and east was the original coniferous forest. Of course, lumbering, farming, and fire have made such changes that the original areas are now hard to identify.

3

Also the borders were often poorly defined, there being local areas in which the types were mingled.

The topography of the state is generally flat or rolling, with two notable exceptions. In the southeastern part of the state the streams have cut deeply, and there are many cliffs and bluffs, which reach their extreme in the very bold bluffs along the Mississippi River. In the northern part of Cook County, in the northeastern part of the state, there are also high cliffs and bluffs. Locally there is also considerable relief, along the St. Croix River, the Minnesota River, and the shore of Lake Superior.

All of the state, except a small area in the southeast adjacent to the Mississippi River, was covered by ice during the Glacial Period. The action of the ice and the morainal deposits from it were responsible for the abundant lakes, marshes, bogs, and swamps.

Of the calcareous rocks, the limestones and dolomites are distributed primarily in the southeastern part of the state, from Dakota to Fillmore counties and eastward, while slates and basic igneous types are in the northeastern part, from southeastern St. Louis County through all but northern Lake County and nearly all of Cook County. Other local areas occur, especially along the Mississippi River from Scott to Brown counties.

Of the acidic rocks, sandstones occur in the southeastern part of the state, associated with the calcareous deposits and along the Minnesota River; they are replaced westward along the river by acidic igneous types, these extending into Big Stone County. Large areas of quartzite are in Pipestone and the adjacent Rock County and in Cottonwood County and the adjacent Watonwan. There is a large area of acidic igneous rocks in the upper half of St. Louis and in northern Lake counties extending into the extreme northwestern corner of Cook County.

DISTRIBUTION OF THE FERNS

The southeastern part of the state has many species of ferns. Goldie's Fern (*Dryopteris Goldiana*), Silvery Spleenwort (*Athyrium thelypterioides*), Narrow-leaved Spleenwort (*Athyrium pycnocarpon*), Broad Beech-fern (*Thelypteris hexagonoptera*), and a variety of the Fragile Fern (*Cystopteris fragilis* var. *protrusa*) are found only in this region in rich, damp, shady woods. The Walking Fern (*Camptosorus rhizophyllus*), found on shady, moist, limestone rocks, the two Cliff Brakes (*Pellaea glabella* and *P. atropurpurea*) and the Slender Lip-fern (*Cheilanthes Feei*), found on exposed calcareous rocks, are also restricted to this area. Together with the other more widely distributed species, they make the area one of the best in the state for ferns.

The other region in which ferns are especially abundant is the northeastern part of the state, in St. Louis, Lake, and Cook counties. Near Lake Superior there are gorges formed by the streams that flow into the lake, and these and the cliffs along the Canadian border lakes in Cook County harbor many rare species not found elsewhere. These are the Mountain Moss (*Selaginella selaginoides*), Rocky-Mountain Woodsia (*Woodsia scopulina*), Smooth Woodsia (*Woodsia glabella*), Alpine Woodsia (*Woodsia alpina*), Fir Club-moss (*Lycopodium Selago*); the Fragrant Fern (*Dryopteris fragrans*), the Northern Oak-fern (*Gymnocarpium Robertianum*), and a variety of the Spinulose Shield-fern (*Dryopteris spinulosa* var. *americana*) are confined to this region except for a single station for each farther south.

Several other species occur in the northeastern part of the state, but they are more widespread than the ones discussed above. They occur chiefly in the region of the original coniferous forest, east and north of Lake of the Woods, Beltrami, Cass, Aitkin, and Pine counties. Such species are several of the Club Mosses (*Lycopodium annotinum, L. clavatum, L. complanatum,* and *L. dendroideum*), the Oak Fern (*Gymnocarpium Dryopteris*), the Long Beech-fern (*Thelypteris Phegopteris*), and the Dwarf Scouring-rush (*Equisetum scirpoides*).

Few species grow in the prairie area except in locally sheltered places. The only characteristic species of the prairie are the Hairy Pepperwort (*Marsilea mucronata*) and the Prairie Quillwort (*Isoëtes melanopoda*), which are confined to that area. Several of the species of Horsetails (*Equisetum laevigatum* and *E. hyemale*) grow in the prairie as well as in other areas.

A number of species are quite widespread and occur throughout the state or are absent only in parts of the prairie area. These are the Rock Spike-moss (*Selaginella rupestris*), Field Horsetail (*Equisetum arvense*), the Ostrich Fern (*Matteuccia Struthiopteris*), the Fragile Fern (*Cystopteris fragilis*), the Bracken (*Pteridium aquilinum*), the Lady Fern (*Athyrium Filix-femina*), and the Spinulose Shield-fern (*Dryopteris spinulosa*).

FERNS IN THE GARDEN

The attractive and practical qualities of ferns make them desirable garden plants. They can be effectively used for green backgrounds, foundation plantings, evergreen cover for shaded areas and in rock gardens. A small area devoted exclusively to ferns can be a special feature of a garden that retains its appeal from the time the first leaves uncoil until autumn. Some species have leaves that are evergreen through the winter or persistent fertile leaves of interesting form. It is especially rewarding to establish a living collection so that the growth and development of the plants can be observed throughout the seasons.

The chief requirements for the cultivation of ferns are shade, protection from battering winds, and a moist, loose, loamy soil. Ferns are generally planted higher than most garden plants, for the growing tip that bears the croziers or leaf buds should be slightly above the soil and the rootstock close to the surface. Ferns require moisture but good drainage, except for those that grow in boggy places. They are perennial; once established, they require little maintenance and are not much troubled by insects.

Ferns can be obtained from wild-flower nurseries, which generally carry several different species that are readily cultivated. Plants can be obtained from the wild, especially from areas that are planned for development or from sites where large colonies have been established. When transplanting ferns, a mat of soil around the rootstock should be taken with as little disturbance to the roots as possible. Rare or local species should not be transplanted since they usually do not survive in the garden, and it is important to conserve these natural resources. Although some species from other regions will persist in cultivation distant from their native range, it is well to start with species native to Minnesota. These are most likely to grow successfully, especially if their native habitat is replicated as closely as possible. A selection of native species and descriptions of their qualities that make them appropriate for the garden follow, according to their size and habit.

Tall Plants—2½ to 4 Feet

The Cinnamon fern (*Osmunda cinnamomea*) and the Interrupted fern (*Osmunda Claytoniana*) are suitable for foundation plantings. These are large species with handsome crowns of leaves that can also serve as background plantings for flowers, along walls, or as tall ground cover in shaded places. The Royal fern (*Osmunda regalis*) is also large and the entire, ultimate segments of the leaves are quite distinct from the other species. The Royal fern requires moisture and grows best in wet soil at the edge of a pool. The Osmundas have an erect stem or a slow-growing creeping one; thus the plants will remain near the place they are planted for many years. Ostrich fern (*Matteuccia Struthiopteris*) is one of the handsome ferns, for it forms dense crowns of tall leaves. It grows well in shade or sunny places and will tolerate quite moist sites. The fertile leaves persist through the winter and make attractive dried arrangements. This is the most prized of the ferns for culinary purposes; the young leaf buds are prepared much as asparagus is. The Ostrich fern grows well around foundations, but the rootstock produces runners that form new crowns. Bracken (*Pteridium aquilinum*) is too large and rampant for the usual garden but may be used where there is sufficient room. It usually grows well in any habitat and forms a dense colony providing shelter for wildlife. The old leaves are resistant to decay and form a persistent tangle on the ground.

Medium to Tall Plants—1½ to 2 Feet

Spinulose Shield-fern (*Dryopteris spinulosa*) can be used in the same manner as the Ostrich fern where a smaller scale is appropriate. The Crested fern (*Dryopteris cristata*) also has an erect habit but is suitable for wet sites. These species have short, creeping stems and will persist for many years close to their original site. Lady fern (*Athyrium Filix-femina*) forms clumps of more delicately divided leaves that make a handsome background planting. The leaves are easily damaged by wind, and the lower portions may become ragged-looking in the summer. Maidenhair (*Adiantum pedatum*) is especially desirable in shaded, moist, areas, protected from the wind. The blackish petioles make a particularly fine contrast to the delicate green color of the leaves. These plants form dense colonies with age, especially in neutral or somewhat calcareous soils. Rattlesnake fern (*Botrychium virginianum*) is somewhat smaller and produces only a single leaf each season. The fertile apical portion is bright yellow when the spores are mature contrasting with the pale green of the sterile leaf. It is difficult to grow and more of a novelty than other garden ferns.

Small Plants—½ to 1½ Feet

The Long Beech-fern (*Thelypteris Phegopteris*) and the Oak fern (*Gymnocarpium Dryopteris*) form extensive colonies with their widely creeping stems. They require shade or only partial sun and loamy soils. The Marsh Fern (*Thelypteris palustris*) occurs in wet, open sites or semishade and will form dense colonies around the edge of ponds. The Sensitive fern (*Onoclea sensilibis*) occurs naturally in wet sites but appears to be tolerant of drier places and is well worth trying in any niche. It forms special fertile leaves with bead-like segments that persist through the winter and shed spores early in the year, often on snow in late winter. The persistent fertile leaves are attractive in dried bouquets.

Rock Garden Ferns

The Fragile fern (*Cystopteris fragilis*) is adapted for a variety of rocky shaded places and its relative, the Bulblet fern (*C. bulbifera*), also grows well in the garden but requires calcareous, moist, shaded rocks. Slender Cliff-brake (*Cryptogramma Stelleri*) also grows on wet, calcereous rocks and is less commonly grown in the garden. The leaves develop early in the spring and especially the fertile ones often wither during the summer. Rusty Woodsia (*Woodsia ilvensis*) is one of the best of the ferns for rock gardens, forming tufts of scaly leaves in crevices. It requires acidic conditions for its best growth. Common Polypody (*Polypodium virginianum*) has evergreen leaves and is especially desirable for rock gardens. Its leaves respond to changes in winter temperature. In moderately cold weather, as low as $25°$ F, the leaves are expanded, but they become curled in colder temperatures and expand again as the temperature moderates. Mats of the Common Polypody should be planted on or among rocks, upon which some humus has accumulated, with the stem apex free to creep on the rock surface.

Fern Allies in the Garden

These plants are only distantly related to ferns, and they have unusual forms that add interest to the garden. They are especially difficult to transplant. The Running Club-moss (*Lycopodium clavatum*) and the Ground Cedar (*Lycopodium complanatum*) have wide creeping stems and grow in light litter, in moist, acid soils, in shade. The Water Horsetail (*Equisetum fluviatile*) is especially attractive at the edge of a pool and the Wood Horsetail (*Equisetum sylvaticum*) will form dense colonies in acid soils in shady wood.

PREPARATION OF A HERBARIUM

Persons who develop a more than casual interest in the study of ferns and their identification will want to prepare a permanent record of their finds. A collection of pressed and dried specimens suitably mounted and labeled will make these specimens available for study during the winter months and will also make possible detailed observation and dissection, usually not convenient in the field. The herbarium also will be useful for the comparison and identification of future collections.

Ferns are best collected in a field press of some kind so that they may be pressed at once. A collecting can or vasculum may be used, but many species will wilt and may not be in good condition when taken out for pressing at the end of the day. The usual field press consists of two wooden frames about 12 by 18 inches with two cardboards as backing and sheets of newspaper between to receive the specimens. Straps or rope will close the press under pressure. Many variants are possible; a large magazine will suffice if necessary. The specimens must be kept under pressure until they are dry, but excessive pressure should be avoided. Each sheet of specimens may be placed between sheets of blotting paper, and pressure may be maintained by tying the press or placing weights on top. The blotters should be changed frequently until the plants are air dry. In this condition they will keep indefinitely as long as they are stored in a dry place and mice and insects are kept out. Ferns as a rule, however, are not particularly susceptible to insect damage. At the time of collecting, notes should be taken that will later be written on a label to go with the mounted specimen. These notes should include locality, state, county, and distance from the nearest town; habitat data, such as the nature of the soil, the type of rock, and the degree of shade; the date of collection, the name of the collector; and the names of other species of plants with which the fern was growing. For easier reference it is convenient to number each collection in consecutive order.

When the spcimens are dried, they may be taped or glued to a sheet of white paper, and the label, about 3 by 5 inches or less, attached in one corner, preferably the lower right. The standard size for mounting sheets is 16½ by 11½ inches. Of course, only one collection of a species should be mounted on a sheet. The sheets may then be placed in folders and filed in a box or cabinet, arranged according to their classification. If in doubt about the identity of a specimen, the collector may send it, with a label, to the Herbarium, Department of Botany, University of Minnesota, Biological Sciences Center, St. Paul, Minnesota 55108, and the name will be supplied. Such specimens should be collected in duplicate so that the collector may retain one and the Herbarium the other.

THE AMERICAN FERN SOCIETY

The American Fern Society has over four hundred members, including many besides professional botanists. Its periodical, the *American Fern Journal*, carries articles covering all phases of fern study: gardening, culture of young ferns, distribution information, keys to groups, descriptions of new forms, varieties and species, and field observations. Members may exchange information and specimens through notices in the *Journal* and may also borrow fern books and specimens from the Society's Library and Herbarium. Correspondence concerning membership may be addressed to the American Fern Society, United States National Herbarium, NHB No. 166, Smithsonian Institution, Washington, D. C. 20560.

USE OF THIS HANDBOOK

Tentative identification of a specimen is possible simply by referring to the illustrations. The keys are designed as an aid to positive identification. In most cases a 10X or a 15X hand lens will be needed to see clearly some of the characters used. Special dissection will be necessary in a few cases. The keys have been constructed to make the identification as easy as possible, but the variation in many species frequently necessitates, for accuracy, the use of some of the less obvious but more stable characters.

The keys consist of pairs of headings, the specimen to be compared to each of the two statements and then keyed further under the heading that fits it better. A statement heading either will refer to another pair of choices or will name the plant. The specimen may then be compared with the illustrations and the discussion of the characters under that species. Success in using the keys depends upon careful and accurate observation.

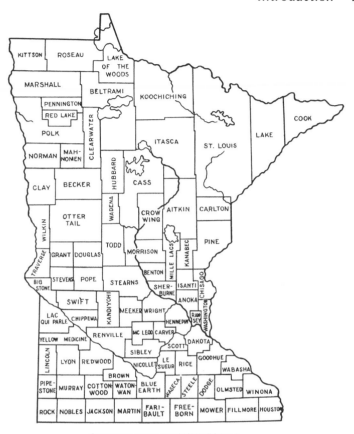

COUNTY MAP OF MINNESOTA

The maps of distribution within the state have been prepared from the collection of ferns in the Herbarium of the Department of Botany of the University of Minnesota. Collections that could not be accurately plotted on the maps were not used. The dots all represent the actual place of collection of the specimens. In some cases several collections from localities close to each other are covered by a single dot on the map.

It is apparent that the distribution of many species in the state is not completely known, and many new county records will be added by additional collecting. Those who collect a species in a county that the map does not include in the presently known range may send a specimen to the Herbarium (address given above), and they will materially aid in the accumulation of knowledge about the distribution of our native flora.

The statements of general range of the species have been drawn from Britton and Brown, *Illustrated Flora*, and from Gray's *Manual*. The common or vernacular names used have been taken from those listed by Una F. Weatherby, "The English Names of North American Ferns," *American Fern Journal* 42:134-151, 1952. However, local names used by people in the state may be quite different. The variation in the application of common names, some species having several and some names referring to several species, makes it desirable to use the Latin names whenever referring to a plant. These change too, for various technical reasons, but in most discussions the changes are cross-referenced so that the application is clear. In this handbook, after the accepted name the synonyms or equivalent names in use in Gray's *Manual* and Britton and Brown's *Illustrated Flora* are given in brackets.

A few marginal species, varieties, and forms are included in this handbook—those that may be expected to occur in Minnesota but have not yet been discovered. Where species show variations, the best-marked geographic varieties are treated under separate headings; varieties and forms of lesser value are treated in the body of the text.

A centimeter rule is reproduced below to enable anyone studying the ferns to visualize more readily the dimensions given in the keys.

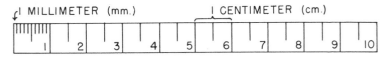

ENTIRE   SCALE = I DECIMETER

10 mm. = I cm.   10 cm. = I dm.   10 dm. = I meter (mm.)

THE   METRIC   SCALE

ILLUSTRATED GLOSSARY

Four plates have been prepared to illustrate the technical terms used in this book. Two of these follow the key to the families and illustrate terms used in the treatments of the Adder's-tongue family, Flowering

Fern family, and Polypody family. The third plate follows the key to the species in the Horsetail family, and the fourth precedes the key to the species in the Club Moss family.

BIBLIOGRAPHY

The following list of books will serve as an introduction to other publications on ferns. The two basic references are Gray's *Manual*, by M. L. Fernald, and *The New Britton and Brown, Illustrated Flora*, by H. A. Gleason (Pteridophytes by C. V. Morton).

A comparison between the fern treatments in the two books just mentioned, as well as in others cited below, and this book on Minnesota ferns will reveal a number of cases in which the authors do not agree on the classification or on the names of the same ferns. It must be realized that, in spite of considerable study, many of the problems of classification are not finally solved, and diverse opinions are likely to exist until the time when sufficient evidence is at hand. In most cases a difference in names is due to a difference in classification, but in some it is entirely a matter of the application of the International Rules of Botanical Nomenclature. In some examples, the application of the rules is not entirely certain, and differences of interpretation arise.

American Fern Journal, a quarterly published by the American Fern Society (see p. 10).

Billington, C., *Ferns of Michigan*. Cranbrook Institute of Science, 1952.

Clute, W. N., *Our Ferns, Their Haunts, Habits and Folklore*. Ed. 2. Frederick Stokes Company, New York, 1938.

Cooperrider, T. S. *The Ferns and Other Pteridophytes of Iowa*. State Univ. of Iowa Studies in Nat. Hist. 20 (1). 1959.

Fernald, M. L., *Gray's Manual of Botany*. Ed. 8. American Book Co., New York, 1950.

Foster, F. G. *Ferns to Know and Grow*. Hawthorne Books, Inc., New York, 1976.

Gleason, H. A., *The New Britton and Brown, Illustrated Flora of the Northeastern United States and Adjacent Canada*. Vol. 1. New York Botanical Garden, New York, 1952.

Hoshizaki, B. J. *Fern Growers Manual*. Alfred A. Knopf, New York, 1975.

Mohlenbrock, R. H. *The Illustrated Flora of Illinois — Ferns*. Southern Illinois University Press, Carbondale, Ill., 1967.

Rydberg, P. A., *Flora of the Prairies and Plains of Central North America*. New York Botanical Garden, New York, 1932.

Tryon, R. M., Jr., N. C. Fassett, D. W. Dunlop, and M. E. Diemer, *The Ferns and Fern Allies of Wisconsin*. Ed. 2. University of Wisconsin Press, Madison, 1953.

14 Introduction

ACKNOWLEDGMENTS

The author is indebted to Miss Wilma Monserud for her excellent and painstaking work on the illustrations and to Mrs. Agnes Forsberg for aid in the preparation of the distribution maps and in typing the manuscript. Dr. A. O. Dahl, Dr. E. C. Abbe, and Dr. G. B. Ownbey have been helpful in many matters relating to the publication.

Much of the preliminary field work and writing of the manuscript was supported by grants-in-aid from the Graduate School of the University of Minnesota.

Collecting since the first edition has added many distribution records and three species, *Asplenium platyneuron, Polystichum acrostichoides,* and *Polystichum Braunii,* to the recorded state flora. Because extensive late manuscript changes would have been necessary had I included these species in the keys, they are not keyed out but are treated at the ends of their respective genera.

Among botanists who have added most significantly to recent knowledge of the ferns and fern allies of Minnesota are W. H. Wagner and his students during several periods at the Lake Itasca Biological Sessions; G. B. Ownbey and several student advisees who have collected over most of the state; J. Beitel, *Lycopodium* specialist who has collected extensively in the northern part of the state; and J. H. Peck, working in the southeastern counties where he found two species new to the state. The new distribution maps, prepared for this edition by Dr. Ownbey, reflect the efforts of all of these individuals. As in the first edition, each dot on the maps is represented by one or more voucher specimens permanently preserved in the University of Minnesota Herbarium. The color photographs, with minor exceptions, are the work of Audrey Engels. Finally, publication assistance was provided by the Junior F. Hayden Fund, University of Minnesota.

INTRODUCTION TO THE SECOND EDITION

This revision of *The Ferns and Fern Allies of Minnesota* contains the changes in nomenclature and classification that are needed to reflect our modern knowledge of the plants. It does not incorporate the many cytological and other detailed studies on North American ferns that have been conducted in the years since the first publication. This would have required much more space and a technical treatment beyond the needs of a manual for identification that provides ecological and geographic information.

Rolla Tryon

Pteridophyta

The ferns and fern allies comprise the plant phylum Pteridophyta, comparable to the seed plants (Spermatophyta), mosses (Bryophyta), and algae, fungi, and lichens (Thallophyta). A more recent classification places all the ferns and fern allies in the same phylum as the seed plants (Tracheophyta) but in separate groups under it. In any case, these spore-bearing vascular plants form a traditional and practical group.

In Minnesota there are 9 families of Pteridophytes, including a total of 26 genera and 72 species. In addition to the species, the varieties, forms, and hybrids make a total of 98 different kinds included in this handbook as native to the state. Ten ferns that occur in adjacent states and may be expected to be found in Minnesota are also treated.

KEY TO FAMILIES

1. Leaves with stipes (as in Fig. 1) except in a few species (Fig. 2) in which the stem is very short and thickened, leaves large, more than 3 cm. long and usually much longer, alternate, borne on a subterranean or epigeous stem 2
   2. Leaves with evident stipes (as in Fig. 1), pinnately divided (Fig. 3) or rarely entire, the sterile and usually the fertile broadly expanded 3
      3. Plant with an erect subterranean stem; roots fleshy; sporangia borne in spikes or panicles on a specialized fertile branch of the leaf (Figs. 1, 4) . . . .**Ophioglossaceae** (p. 21)
      3. Plant with a short- or long-creeping rhizome, usually at or near the surface of the soil; roots fibrous; sporangia borne on fertile pinnae of the leaf (as in Fig. 5) or on completely fertile leaves (Fig. 6, segment of such) 4

15

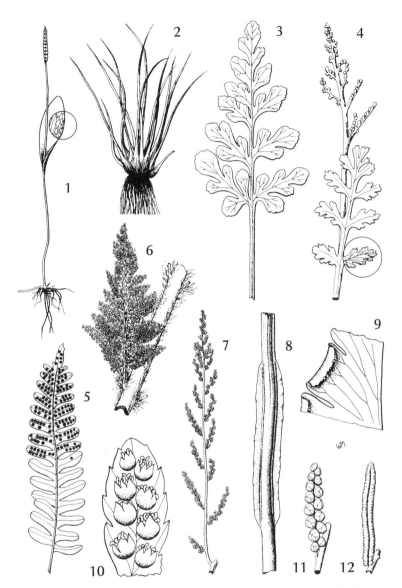

FIGURE 1. *Ophioglossum vulgatum*, plant. FIGURE 2. *Isoëtes*, plant. FIGURE 3. *Cryptogramma Stelleri*, sterile leaf. FIGURE 4. *Botrychium matricariifolium*, leaf. FIGURE 5. *Polypodium virginianum*, leaf. FIGURE 6. *Osmunda cinnamomea*, fertile pinna. FIGURE 7. *Osmunda regalis*, fertile pinna. FIGURE 8. *Osmunda*, base of stipe. FIGURE 9. *Adiantum pedatum*, portion of fertile pinnule. FIGURE 10. *Cystopteris fragilis*, segment. FIGURE 11. *Onoclea sensibilis*, fertile pinna. FIGURE 12. *Matteuccia Struthiopteris*, fertile pinna.

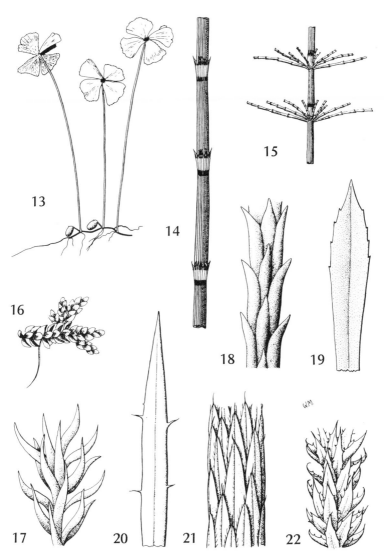

FIGURE 13. *Marsilea mucronata*, plant. FIGURE 14. *Equisetum*, portion of stem.
FIGURE 15. *Equisetum*, portion of stem. FIGURE 16. *Azolla mexicana*, plant.
FIGURE 17. *Lycopodium*, portion of branch. FIGURE 18. *Lycopodium*, portion
of branch. FIGURE 19. *Lycopodium lucidulum*, leaf. FIGURE 20. *Lycopodium
inundatum*, leaf. FIGURE 21. *Selaginella rupestris*, portion of stem.
FIGURE 22. *Selaginella selaginoides*, portion of stem.

18   Pteridophyta

4. Sporangia naked, borne on completely fertile (not vegetative) segments (Figs. 6, 7); leaves with stipules at the very base of the stipe) (Fig. 8) . . . . **Osmundaceae** (p. 33)

4. Sporangia usually covered by an indusium (Figs. 9, 10) borne on the backs of little-modified vegetative segments or enclosed in highly modified inrolled segments (Figs. 11, 12); leaves without stipules . . . . **Polypodiaceae** (p. 40)

2. Leaves awl-shaped and sessile (Fig. 2) or with long stipes and the blade divided, clover-like, into four fan-shaped segments (Fig. 13) 5

5. Leaves with a long stipe, the blade divided, clover-like, into four fan-shaped segments, leaves arising at intervals from a creeping stem (Fig. 13). . . . . **Marsileaceae** (p. 38)

5. Leaves awl-shaped, sessile, arising in a rosette from a thickened, corm-like stem (Fig. 2). . . . . **Isoetaceae** (p. 153)

1. Leaves sessile, small, about 2 cm. long or shorter; whorled or alternate, borne on elongated aerial or aquatic branches of the stem (Figs. 14-22) 6

6. Leaves and frequently also branches borne in whorls at the nodes of the jointed and longitudinally grooved stem (Figs. 14, 15). . . . . **Equisetaceae** (p. 114)

6. Leaves alternate, stem not jointed nor longitudinally grooved . . 7

7. Leaves disposed in a single plane, with an upper and a lower lobe; free-floating, small (up to 2 cm. long) aquatic plants (Fig. 16) . . . . **Salviniaceae** (p. 38)

7. Leaves disposed in two or more planes, not divided into lobes; terrestrial plants mostly 10 cm. or more tall 8

8. Vegetative leaves mostly smooth on the margin (Figs. 17, 18) occasionally with small, irregular ascending teeth (Fig. 19); or if prominently toothed, then the leaf long-lanceolate (Fig. 20) . . . . **Lycopodiaceae** (p. 134)

8. Vegetative leaves with hairs on the margin (Fig. 21) or with a few prominent teeth disposed nearly at right angles to the margin and the leaf lanceolate-ovate (Fig. 22). . . . . **Selaginellaceae** (p. 150)

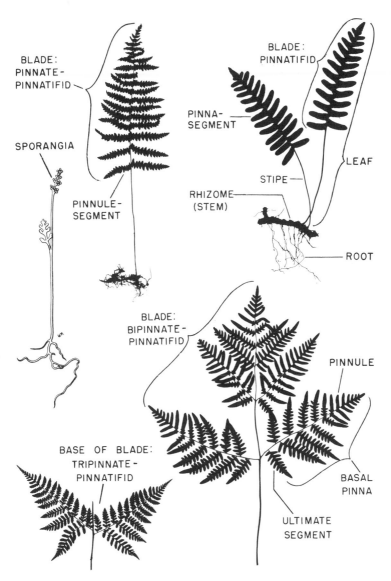

GLOSSARY PLATE 1. The complexity of the leaves of true ferns has given rise to a special terminology which is useful in referring to the different types of leaves and their parts. These terms are illustrated on this and the following plate.

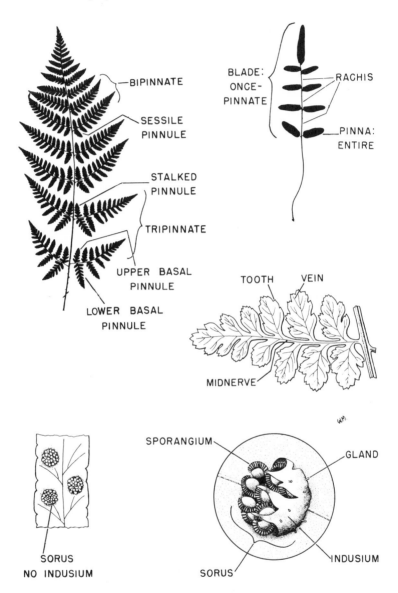

GLOSSARY PLATE 2. Additional terms referring to the leaves of true ferns are
illustrated here. Terms used when referring to the spore-bearing parts
(the sporangia) and associated features are also illustrated.

True Ferns

ADDER'S-TONGUE FAMILY, Ophioglossaceae

Roots fleshy; stem short, erect, subterranean, bearing a single leaf (rarely more) divided into a fertile spike or panicle and a sterile expanded blade; leaves folded in the bud; sporangia large, naked, sessile or nearly so; spores of one kind. (Glossary Plate 1, p. 19)

KEY TO GENERA

1. Veins free; blade, with rare exception, divided; sporangia (except in dwarf plants) borne in a panicle (Fig. 23). . . . . *Botrychium* (p. 21)
1. Veins forming a network; blade entire; sporangia borne in a spike (Fig. 24) . . . . *Ophioglossum* (p. 32)

Botrychium Sw.

Leaves one to a plant (with rare exceptions); the sterile portion (blade) pinnately divided, sometimes merely lobed or rarely entire, veins free; the fertile portion an elongate stalk branching in the upper part to form a panicle bearing the sporangia (rarely in dwarf plants this is reduced to a spike).

A genus of seven species in Minnesota, but only one of them, *B. virginianum*, is at all common. This is characterized by its large, lacy blade. The others are all rare, some very rare. Among many of them there is considerable variation in leaf cutting. At least some of this is dependent upon the age of the plant and the growing conditions. See Weatherby, C. A., *Amer. Fern Journ.* 25:47-51, 95-97, 1935, for the named minor variations.

21

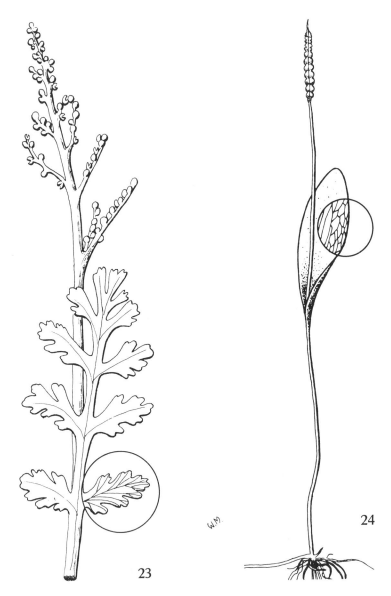

FIGURE 23. *Botrychium matricariifolium*, leaf. FIGURE 24.
Ophioglossum vulgatum var. *pseudopodum*, plant.

KEY TO SPECIES*

1. Blade long-stalked, the stalk about as long as the blade, with a whitish margin on the segments (under magnification) (Fig. 25); leaf arising in midsummer, the blade wintering over and often persisting until the next leaf is produced 2
   2. Most of the ultimate segments ovate, not more than twice as long as broad; pinnae lobed nearly to the tip (Fig. 26) . . . .
   . . . . B. multifidum (p. 25)
   2. Blade cut in a lacy manner (Fig. 27) *or* most of the ultimate segments lanceolate, more than twice as long as broad; pinnae not lobed near their tip, ending in a rather long, entire segment (Fig. 28) . . . . B. dissectum (p. 26)
1. Blade sessile or short-stalked on fertile leaves, the stalk usually much shorter than the blade, without a whitish margin; leaf arising in the spring, withering by autumn 3
   3. Blade short-stalked in fertile leaves, or if sessile, then the blade oblong 4
      4. Blade once pinnate with 2 to 5 pairs of fan-shaped pinnae; spores 0.025-0.035 (rarely up to 0.040) mm. in diameter . . . .
      . . . . B. Lunaria (p. 27)
      4. Blade entire or variously divided; if once pinnate, usually with ovate or ovate-lanceolate pinnae; if the pinnae are fan-shaped, the spores 0.035-0.050 mm. in diameter 5
         5. Both fertile and sterile parts of the leaf erect in the bud, † or only the very tip of the sterile folded over the fertile (Fig. 29); blade commonly pinnatifid or pinnate with ovate pinnae; spores 0.035-0.050 mm. in diameter . . . .
         . . . . B. simplex (p. 28)
         5. Upper part of the blade folded over and partly enclosing the fertile portion in the bud (Fig. 30); blade usually pinnate with ovate-oblong pinnae or pinnate-pinnatifid . . . .
         . . . . .B. matricariifolium (p. 29)
   3. Blade broadly triangular, sessile in fertile leaves. 6
      6. Blade cut as in Fig. 31, usually about 5 cm. long . . . .
      . . . . B. lanceolatum (p. 30)

* Adapted from Tryon, Fassett, Dunlop, and Diemer, *The Ferns and Fern Allies of Wisconsin*, Madison, 1940.
† The bud will be found at the very base of the stalk of the leaf and enclosed within it.

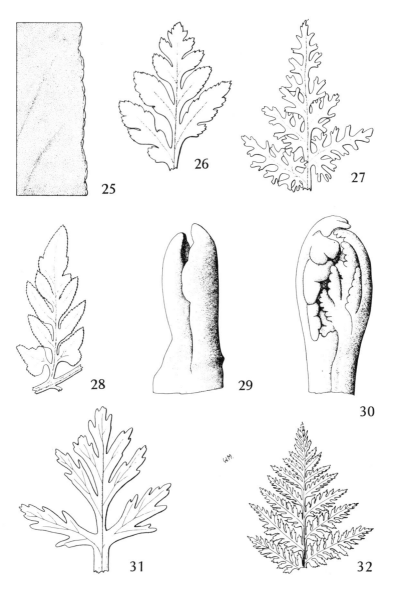

FIGURE 25. *Botrychium multifidum*, margin of blade (magnified). FIGURE 26. *Botrychium multifidum*, tip of pinna. FIGURE 27. *Botrychium dissectum* f. *dissectum*, typical portion of pinna. FIGURE 28. *Botrychium dissectum* f. *obliquum*, pinna. FIGURE 29. *Botrychium simplex*, bud (magnified). FIGURE 30. *Botrychium matricariifolium*, bud (magnified). FIGURE 31. *Botrychium lanceolatum* var. *angustisegmentum*, sterile blade. FIGURE 32. *Botrychium virginianum*, portion of pinna.

6. Blade cut in a lacy manner (Fig. 32), usually well over 10 cm. long . . . .*B. virginianum* (p. 30)

LEATHERY GRAPE-FERN, *Botrychium multifidum* (S. G. Gmel.) Rupr.

This species and the next are distinguished from the others by the long-stalked and persistent blade; *B. multifidum* may be separated from *B. dissectum* by the cutting of the blade. There are two rather well-marked variations.

B. multifidum var. *multifidum*, Map 1, Fig. 33

This has relatively few ultimate segments, which are often crowded and are rounded at the tip, the blade is smaller than in the next variety, being mostly 3-6 cm. long.

It grows in rather open grassy places or in thickets in the central and northeastern parts of the state.

Distribution: Labrador south to Pennsylvania, west to Minnesota; British Columbia; Eurasia.

B. multifidum var. *intermedium* (D. C. Eaton) Farwell, Map 2, Fig. 34

This variety has many ultimate segments, which are not crowded and which mostly have pointed tips. The blade is usually 10-15 cm. or more long.

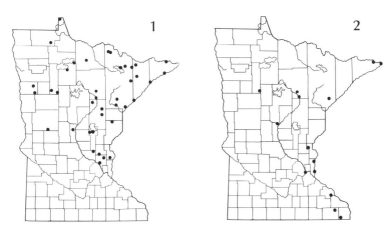

MAP 1. *Botrychium multifidum* var. *multifidum*. MAP 2. *Botrychium multifidum* var. *intermedium*.

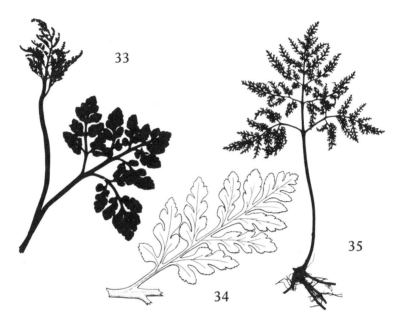

FIGURE 33. *Botrychium multifidum* var. *multifidum*, leaf, 11 cm. long.
FIGURE 34. *Botrychium multifidum* var. *intermedium*, middle pinna,
6.5 cm. long. FIGURE 35. *Botrychium dissectum* f. *dissectum*,
sterile plant, blade 9 cm. long.

Some intermediates occur with the cutting of the blade as in var. *intermedium* but with a small blade or with the cutting of var. *multifidum* but with a large blade.

Var. *intermedium* grows mostly in more shaded places than var. *multifidum*, but sometimes it is found in the open.

Its range is more southerly in Minnesota.

Distribution: New Brunswick to British Columbia, south to Virginia, Iowa, and California.

DISSECTED GRAPE-FERN, *Botrychium dissectum* Spreng., Map 3, Fig. 35

The typical form of this species (f. *dissectum*) is easily recognized by its lacy cutting. It has been collected only twice in the state, but new localities will probably be discovered by careful search. A form that is also very rare in the state is *Botrychium dissectum* f. *obliquum* (Muhl.

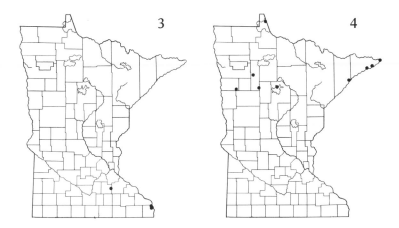

MAP 3. *Botrychium dissectum*. MAP 4. *Botrychium Lunaria*.

ex Willd.) Fernald. This has the segments very finely serrate, but not dissected (Fig. 28 in key).

The collections of this species have been made in both spring and fall in several southeastern counties of the state. It grows in low, shady woods, in rich, organic soil.

Distribution: Nova Scotia south to South Carolina, west to Minnesota and Arkansas.

MOONWORT, *Botrychium Lunaria* (L.) Sw., Map 4

The Moonwort can usually be distinguished by its fan-shaped pinnae, but some forms are very close to some phases of *B. simplex* and can be separated from that species only by the size of the spores. The spores of *B. Lunaria* are 0.025-0.035 (rarely up to 0.040) mm. in diameter, while those of *B. simplex* are 0.035-0.050 mm. in diameter.

The typical Moonwort (var. *Lunaria*) has the pinnae distinctly fan-shaped; they are close together and often overlapping. *B. Lunaria* var. *minganense* (Vict.) Dole has the pinnae rather ovate or obovate, often lobed; several leaves are often produced from the same stem. It was collected once with the typical phase on Garden Island, Lake of the Woods County. *B. Lunaria* var. *onondagense* (Underw.) House (Fig. 36) [*B. Lunaria* f. *gracile* (Schur) Aschers. & Graebn.] has the pinnae distant, sometimes rather oblong, and the blade thinner than in var.

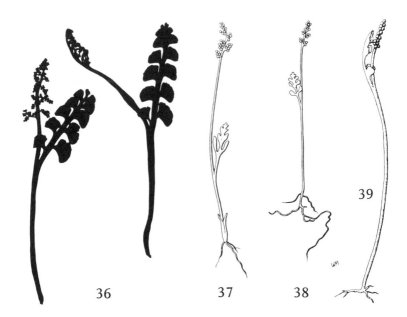

FIGURE 36. *Botrychium Lunaria* var. *onondagense*, leaves, *left*, 11 cm. long.
FIGURE 37. *Botrychium simplex* var. *simplex*, plant, 14 cm. tall. FIGURE 38.
Botrychium simplex var. *laxifolium*, plant, 12 cm. tall. FIGURE 39.
Botrychium simplex var. *tenebrosum*, plant, 7 cm. tall.

Lunaria. It is probably a shade form; most of our collections are of this
variety.

The Moonwort has been found growing in woods, often on ledges
or mossy talus, in Lake, Cook, and Lake of the Woods counties and in
deciduous woods in Cass, Clearwater, and Norman counties.

Distribution: Greenland to Alaska, south to New York, Minnesota,
Arizona, and California.

SMALL GRAPE-FERN, *Botrychium simplex* Hitchc., Map 5

This species is not well separated from the others by any one charac-
ter except the large spores (0.035-0.050 mm. in diameter). Each leaf
phase can be separated from given phases of the other species, except
that some phases of var. *laxifolium* are very similar to some of *B. Lunaria* and *B. matricariifolium*.

The typical var. *simplex* (Fig. 37) has the blade inserted low on the

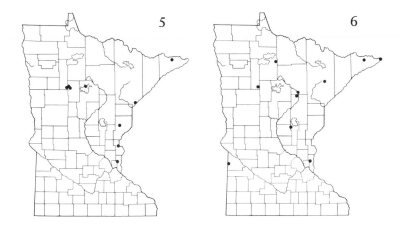

MAP 5. *Botrychium simplex*. MAP 6. *Botrychium matricariifolium*.

stalk, and the basal pinnae are usually larger than the second pair. It grows mostly in open, moist places. *B. simplex* var. *laxifolium* Clausen has the blade inserted about in the middle (Fig. 38) and is once pinnate in well developed leaves. It grows in rather open woods. *B. simplex* var. *tenebrosum* (A. A. Eaton) Clausen has the blade inserted near the tip (Fig. 39) and the blade poorly developed, mostly pinnatifid. It grows in damp, shady woods, sometimes underneath leaves.

The Small Grape-fern is rare and scattered in the state.

Distribution: Newfoundland to British Columbia, south to West Virginia, Indiana, New Mexico, and California; Eurasia.

MATRICARY GRAPE-FERN, *Botrychium matricariifolium* A. Br., Map 6, Fig. 40

The blade with a short stalk separates this species from *B. lanceolatum*, and the folded bud separates it from *B. simplex*. In the few specimens from Minnesota, the blade varies from pinnate to pinnate-pinnatifid.

It grows in woods, usually in damp and shady places.

Distribution: Labrador to Virginia, west to Alberta and Idaho; Eurasia.

LANCE-LEAVED GRAPE-FERN, *Botrychium lanceolatum* (S. G. Gmel.) Rupr. Map 7, Figs. 41, 42

This is a distinct species. The blade is small, and in fertile leaves it is sessile. Also both fertile and sterile parts of the leaf are completely reflexed in the bud (Fig. 42).

It has been collected but once in the state in a brushy, second-growth woods in Mille Lacs County. It probably grows in other deciduous woods in the northeastern part of the state.

Our variety, var. *angustisegmentum* Pease and Moore, ranges from Newfoundland to Minnesota, south to Virginia and Ohio. The more northern var. *lanceolatum* occurs from Labrador to Alaska, south to Maine, Colorado, and Arizona; also in Eurasia.

RATTLESNAKE FERN, *Botrychium virginianum* (L.) Sw., Fig. 43

This is our common species and also one of the most distinctive. The blade is sessile in fertile plants, triangular, and usually larger than in any

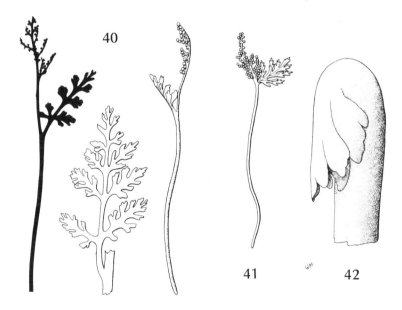

FIGURE 40. *Botrychium matricariifolium,* leaves: *left* blade 3 cm. long, *center* blade 8.5 cm. long, *right* blade 1.5 cm. long. FIGURE 41. *Botrychium lanceolatum* var. *angustisegmentum,* leaf, 13 cm. long. FIGURE 42. *Botrychium lanceolatum* var. *angustisegmentum,* bud (enlarged).

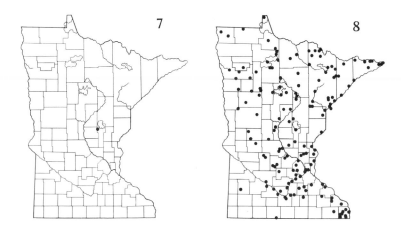

MAP 7. *Botrychium lanceolatum* var. *angustisegmentum*. MAP 8.
Botrychium virginianum var. *virginianum*.

of the other species. In addition the bud at the base of the leaf stalk is not completely enclosed by the sheath but is partly exposed.

Two phases are represented in the state. One, var. *virginianum*, has a thin blade, the segments of it deeply cut and mostly remote (Map 8). The other, *B. virginianum* var. *europaeum* Angstr., has the blade definitely thickened, the segments not so deeply cut and often overlapping.

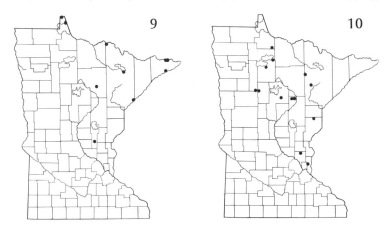

MAP 9. *Botrychium virginianum* var. *europaeum*. MAP 10.
Ophioglossum vulgatum var. *pseudopodum*.

43   44

FIGURE 43. *Botrychium virginianum* var. *virginianum*, leaf, sterile blade
15 cm. long. FIGURE 44. *Ophioglossum vulgatum* var.
pseudopodum, plant, sterile blade 6 cm. long.

This variety is found only in the northern part of the range (Map 9),
where intermediates with var. *virginianum* also occur.

The Rattlesnake fern grows almost throughout the state, in rich,
shady woods or sometimes in thickets or the higher places in bogs.

Distribution: Labrador to British Columbia, south to Florida and
Mexico; Eurasia.

Ophioglossum L.

Leaves usually one to a plant, sometimes several; the sterile portion
generally ovate, undivided, the margin entire, veins forming a network;

the fertile portion an elongate stalk terminating in a spike of sporangia. Represented in Minnesota by a single species.

ADDER'S-TONGUE, *Ophioglossum vulgatum* L., Map 10, Fig. 44

The Adder's-tongue has little resemblance to a fern, even to its relatives the Botrychiums. Perhaps this is the reason it has not been collected more often in the state. Certainly it will not be confused with any other species. Its simple ovate blade with net-venation and its characteristic spike of sporangia are distinctive.

It has been collected in rather open wet sand in several counties. Distribution: Var. *pseudopodum* (Blake) Farwell is widely spread in North America (Quebec to Washington, south to Virginia, Nebraska, and Mexico); var. *pycnostichum* ranges from South Carolina to New Jersey, west to Indiana; and var. *vulgatum* is Eurasian.

FLOWERING FERN FAMILY, Osmundaceae

Roots fibrous; stem a massive compact rhizome, the crown exposed; leaves numerous, pinnate-pinnatifid or bipinnate, large, completely or partially dimorphic, with stipules at the base of the stipe; veins free; leaves coiled in the bud; sporangia relatively large, naked, short-stalked, borne on highly modified pinnae; spores of one kind, green. (Glossary Plates 1 and 2, pp. 19 and 20)

Represented in Minnesota by a single genus.

Osmunda L.

KEY TO SPECIES

1. Leaf entirely fertile, brownish, hairy . . . . . . *O. cinnamomea* (p. 36)
1. Leaf entirely or partly sterile, most of the pinnae green and expanded 2
  2. Blade bipinnate, fertile pinnae, if present, at the apex of the blade
  . . . . *O. regalis* (p. 34)
  2. Blade pinnate-pinnatifid 3
    3. Base of the pinnae nearly smooth or with only a small tuft of hair; margins of the segments smooth; fertile pinnae, if present, in the middle of the blade . . . . *O. Claytoniana* (p. 34)
    3. Base of the pinnae with a definite tuft of hair; margins of the segments with a few hairs (Fig. 51) . . . *O. cinnamomea* (p. 36)

ROYAL FERN, *Osmunda regalis* L., Map 11, Figs. 45, 46

The bipinnate leaves distinguish this species from the others of the genus, as does the fertile blade with the fertile pinnae at the apex. It grows in wet places or rarely in shallow water, both in shade and in sun. It grows in wetter places generally than the other two species. The Royal Fern has been collected in the east-central and northeastern parts of the state.

Distribution: Our representative is var. *spectabilis* (Willd.) A. Gray, from Newfoundland to Florida, west to Saskatchewan and Texas. Other varieties occur in South America, Europe, Africa, and eastern Asia.

INTERRUPTED FERN, *Osmunda Claytoniana* L., Map 12, Figs. 47, 49

The fertile leaf is very distinctive, having the fertile pinnae borne in the middle of the blade. Sterile leaves can be separated from *O. regalis* var. *spectabilis* by their pinnate-pinnatifid rather than bipinnate division, but they are quite similar to the sterile leaves of the next species, *O. cinnamomea*. However, that species has the margins of the segments hairy, while in *O. Claytoniana* they are smooth.

The Interrupted Fern grows in rich, shaded woods, sometimes in open places, usually in drier places than *O. regalis* var. *spectabilis*

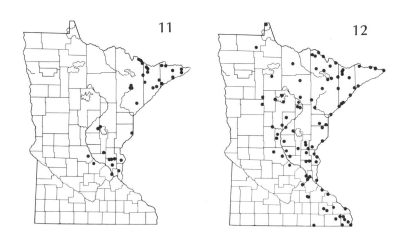

MAP 11. *Osmunda regalis* var. *spectabilis*. MAP 12.
Osmunda Claytoniana.

FIGURE 45. *Osmunda regalis* var. *spectabilis*, sterile leaf, blade 50 cm. long.
FIGURE 46. *Osmunda regalis* var. *spectabilis*, tip of fertile leaf, sterile pinnae 20 cm.
long. FIGURE 47. *Osmunda Claytoniana*, fertile leaf, blade 45 cm. long. FIGURE 48.
Osmunda cinnamomea, fertile leaf, blade 25 cm. long.

and *O. cinnamomea*. It is found generally in the eastern half of the state.

Distribution: Our var. *Claytoniana* occurs from Newfoundland to Manitoba, south to Georgia and Arkansas; var. *vestita* (Wall.) Milde is Himalayan.

CINNAMON FERN, *Osmunda cinnamomea* L., Map 13, Figs. 48,50,51

The leaves of the Cinnamon Fern are similar to those of the Interrupted Fern but may be easily distinguished by the hairs on the margin of the segments. Also there is a much more definite tuft of hairs at the base of each pinna. The sterile leaves are borne in a crown, as in the other species, in the center of which the fertile leaves are borne; these are entirely fertile, brownish, and quite hairy. They die down after the spores are shed and are quite inconspicuous past midsummer.

There are several variations named, but f. *frondosa* (Torr. & Gray) Britt., with part of the leaf fertile and part sterile and green, is the only one that has been collected. Another, f. *incisa* (J. W. Huntington) Gilbert, with lobed pinnule-segments, may well occur in the state, as may f. *auriculata* (Hopkins) Kittredge, with the basal pinnule-segments, particularly the lower ones, greatly elongated and lobed. There is evidence that both these forms may sometimes be a response to severe conditions while the leaves are only partly formed in the buds.

The Cinnamon Fern grows in marshes, wet woods, bogs, or swamps; usually in drier places than *O. regalis* var. *spectabilis* and in wetter ones

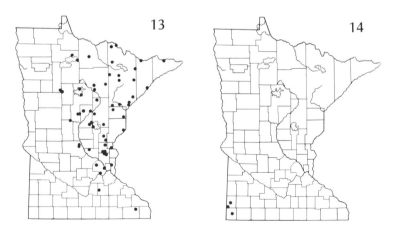

MAP 13. *Osmunda cinnamomea*. MAP 14. *Marsilea mucronata*.

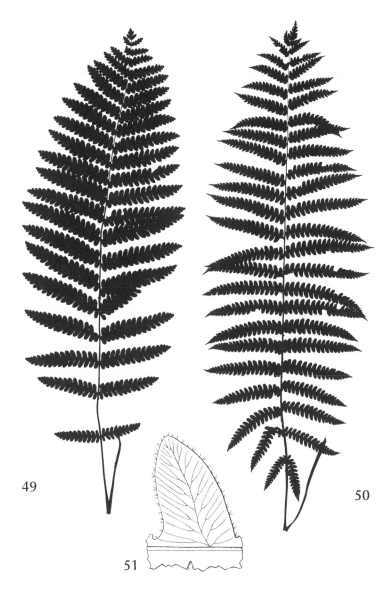

FIGURE 49. *Osmunda Claytoniana*, sterile leaf, blade 60 cm. long. FIGURE 50.
Osmunda cinnamomea, sterile leaf, blade 65 cm. long. FIGURE 51. *Osmunda
cinnamomea*, pinnule-segment of sterile blade, 1 cm. long.

than *O. Claytoniana*. It has been collected in the east, central, and northeastern parts of the state.

Distribution: Our representative is var. *cinnamomea*, from Labrador to Minnesota, south to Florida and Texas; other varieties are in South America and eastern Asia.

WATER CLOVER FAMILY, Marsileaceae

Stem slender, extensively creeping, bearing leaves at intervals; leaves with a long petiole and a blade composed of four fan-shaped pinnae; the highly specialized sporangia-bearing organ, the hairy sporocarp, borne on the rhizome near the base of the leaves; spores of two kinds borne in separate sporangia.

Represented in Minnesota by a single genus and species.

Marsilea L.

HAIRY PEPPERWORT, *Marsilea mucronata* A. Br., Map 14, Fig. 52

This is a very distinctive species; the leaves are hairy and resemble a four-leaved clover.

It has been found in ephemeral prairie pools in the southwestern corner of the state.

Distribution: Saskatchewan to Minnesota, south to Florida and Mexico.

FLOATING FERN FAMILY, Salviniaceae

Plants small, floating, or rooting in wet mud; stem branched; leaves with an upper and a lower lobe; sporocarps in pairs; sporangia highly specialized; spores of two kinds borne in separate sporangia.

Represented in Minnesota by a single genus and species.

Azolla Lam.

MOSQUITO FERN, *Azolla mexicana* Presl, Map. 15, Fig. 53

This fern resembles a small hepatic or moss. It floats on water or may live stranded in wet mud. It is unique and will not be confused with any of the other species by anyone fortunate enough to find it.

52

FIGURE 52. *Marsilea mucronata*, plant, 13 cm. tall.

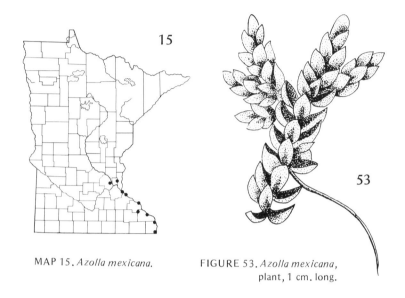

MAP 15. *Azolla mexicana.*

FIGURE 53. *Azolla mexicana,*
plant, 1 cm. long.

It grows in sloughs of the Mississippi River and in a pond near Minneapolis.

Distribution: Minnesota, Wisconsin, Illinois, and Missouri; western United States to South America.

POLYPODY FAMILY, Polypodiaceae

Roots fibrous; stem a compact or extensively creeping rhizome usually at or near the surface of the soil; leaves relatively large, without stipules, coiled in the bud, bearing on the underside small, long-stalked sporangia associated in groups (sori), these usually covered by an indusium, fertile leaves generally similar to the sterile, dimorphic in *Onoclea* and *Matteuccia*; spores of one kind. (Glossary Plates 1 and 2, pp. 19 and 20)

Our largest family, represented by 17 genera and 34 species.

KEY TO GENERA

1. Stipe divided at its tip into two rachises; blade fan-shaped, the pinnae arising from only one side of the rachis-branch (Fig. 54);

indusium formed by a marginal flap covering the sporangia (Fig. 55)
.................................*Adiantum* (p. 56)
1. Stipe and rachis single; pinnae arising from both sides of the rachis 2
2. Veins forming a network (as in Fig. 56) except in the fertile blade of *Onoclea*, which has the sori enclosed by the inrolled segments (Fig. 57) and the basal pinnae not much smaller than the largest ones 3
   3. Sterile blade deeply pinnatifid to pinnate-pinnatifid at the base (Fig. 58); fertile blade bipinnate, each pinnule inrolled to form a "ball" enclosing the sporangia (Fig. 57). . . . *Onoclea* (p. 70)
   3. Sterile and fertile blade entire, usually long and tapering at the tip and heart-shaped at the base (Fig. 59); indusium oblong to linear, attached at one side (Fig. 60) . . . *Camptosorus* (p. 108)
2. Veins free (as in Fig. 61); in *Matteuccia* the sori are enclosed by the inrolled segments (Fig. 62) and the basal pinnae are much reduced 4
   4. Blade gradually tapering to a very narrow base, the basal pinnae at most no more than one-fifth as long as the longest ones (Fig. 63); fertile pinnae inrolled to enclose the sporangia (Fig. 62)· .... *Matteuccia* (p. 66)
   4. Blade not greatly narrowed at the base, the basal pinnae at least one-third as long as the longest ones; sporangia exposed, not enclosed by inrolled segments 5
      5. Stipe and rachis dark brown to almost black..........6
         6. Blade abruptly pinnate at the tip (Fig. 64); sporangia marginal, covered by a continuous marginal flap (Fig. 65)
         ....*Pellaea* (p. 53)
         6. Blade tapering evenly to the tip 7
            7. Blade without hairs, at the most with a few scattered scales; sori borne near the midvein (Fig. 66); indusium oblong to linear, attached at one side (Fig. 67) .....
            .... *Asplenium* (p. 106)
            7. Blade conspicuously hairy (Fig. 68); sori marginal . . .
            .... *Cheilanthes* (p. 53)
      5. Stipe and lower half of the rachis straw-colored to dark brown, at least the upper half of the rachis light brown to greenish..............................8
         8. Blade deeply pinnatifid (Fig. 69), the pinna-segments

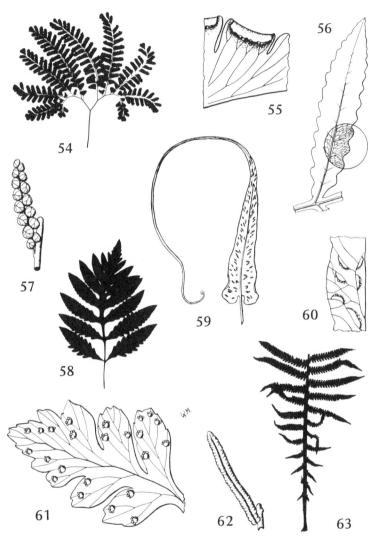

FIGURE 54. *Adiantum pedatum*, leaf. FIGURE 55. *Adiantum pedatum*, portion of fertile pinnule. FIGURE 56. *Onoclea sensibilis*, pinna of sterile leaf. FIGURE 57. *Onoclea sensibilis*, pinna of fertile leaf. FIGURE 58. *Onoclea sensibilis*, sterile leaf. FIGURE 59. *Camptosorus rhizophyllus*, fertile leaf. FIGURE 60. *Camptosorus rhizophyllus*, portion of fertile leaf. FIGURE 61. *Cystopteris*, fertile pinnule. FIGURE 62. *Matteuccia Struthiopteris*, pinna of fertile leaf.
FIGURE 63. *Matteuccia Struthiopteris*, base of sterile leaf.

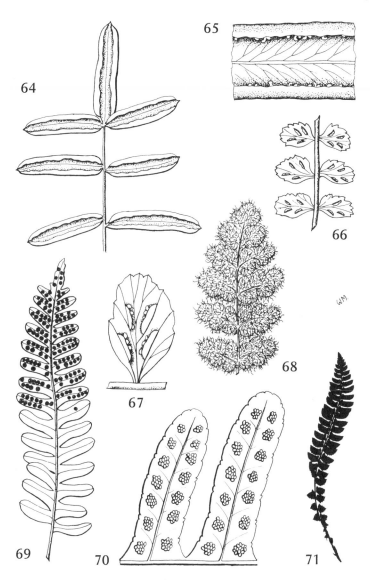

FIGURE 64. *Pellaea*, upper portion of leaf. FIGURE 65. *Pellaea*, portion of fertile pinna. FIGURE 66. *Asplenium Trichomanes*, portion of fertile leaf. FIGURE 67. *Asplenium Trichomanes*, fertile pinna. FIGURE 68. *Cheilanthes Feei*, pinna. FIGURE 69. *Polypodium virginianum*, fertile leaf. FIGURE 70. *Polypodium virginianum*, fertile pinna. FIGURE 71. *Polystichum Lonchitis*, leaf 16 cm. long.

very shallowly toothed; sori round; indusium absent
(Fig. 70) . . . . *Polypodium* (p. 113)
8. Blade once or more than once pinnate or the blade deeply
pinnatifid and the pinna-segments deeply pinnatifid. . .9
9. Blade once pinnate, the pinna margins beset with
bristly teeth (Fig. 71); sori round; indusium umbrella-
shaped, attached at its center. . . . .
. . . . *Polystichum Lonchitis* (p. 72)
9. Blade usually more than once pinnate, if once pinnate
then the pinna margins smooth or blunt-toothed. . 10
10. Indusium formed by a nearly continuous marginal flap (Fig. 72, 73) 11
11. Leaf large, usually 10 dm. or more long;
margins of the fertile and sterile segments recurved; the segments usually hairy on the
midnerve beneath, and broadened at the
base. (Figs. 72, 74) . . . . .*Pteridium* (p. 49)
11. Frond small, usually less than 2 dm. long;
margins of the fertile leaves recurved, of the
sterile leaves flat; segments glabrous and narrowed at the base (Figs. 73, 75, 76) . . . . . .
. . . . *Cryptogramma* (p. 49)
10. Indusium not marginal, variously shaped and
borne on the under surface of the segment, or indusium absent .12
12. Indusium present 13
13. Indusium heart-shaped, attached at the
sinus (Fig. 77) 14
14. Rhizome compact, stout, rachis not
hairy, blades bipinnate or more
highly divided. . *Dryopteris* (p. 72)
14. Rhizome slender, rachis hairy,
blades pinnate-pinnatifid . . . .
. . . . *Thelypteris*
palustris var. *pubescens*   (p. 89)
13. Indusium various; if strongly hooked
and apparently heart-shaped, attached
along the inner side (Fig. 78) 15
15. Indusium attached beneath the

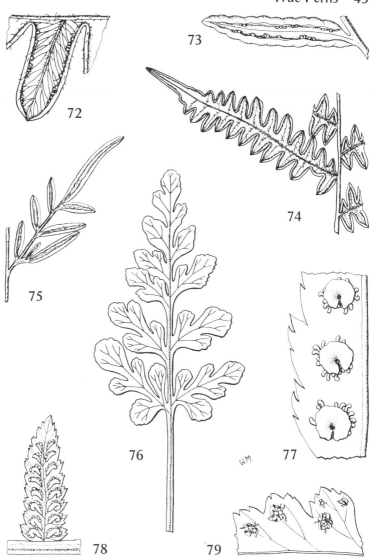

FIGURE 72. *Pteridium aquilinum* var. *latiusculum*, fertile segment. FIGURE 73. *Cryptogramma Stelleri*, fertile pinnule. FIGURE 74. *Pteridium aquilinum* var. *latiusculum*, portion of fertile pinna. FIGURE 75. *Cryptogramma Stelleri*, fertile pinna. FIGURE 76. *Cryptogramma Stelleri*, sterile leaf. FIGURE 77. *Dryopteris spinulosa*, portion of fertile segment. FIGURE 78. *Athyrium Filix-femina* var. *Michauxii*, fertile pinnule. FIGURE 79. *Woodsia oregana*, portion of fertile segment.

sorus, its thread- or scale-like segments curving over it (Fig. 79); small tufted rock plants frequently hairy or scaly beneath . . . . *Woodsia* (p. 58)

15. Indusium entire or split only at the tip, attached at one side and arching over the sorus or attached at its center 16

16. Sori roundish; indusium cup-shaped attached at one side (Fig. 80), or umbrella-shaped and attached at its center (Fig. 81). 17

17. Indusium cup-shaped, attached at one side and arching over the sporangia; blade thin, deciduous, not scaly beneath or very slightly so; segments not bristly-toothed (Fig. 80). . . . . . *Cystopteris* (p. 100)

17. Indusium umbrella-shaped, attached at its center (Fig. 81); blade evergreen, leathery, definitely scaly beneath; segments with bristly teeth (Fig. 82). . . . . *Polystichum Braunii* var. *Purshii* (p. 70)

16. Sori elongated, sometimes hooked (horseshoe-shaped); indusium elongate, or curved, attached along one side (Figs. 78, 83, 84). . *Athyrium* (p. 96)

12. Indusium absent or apparently so (where the indusium is early-deciduous or becomes inconspicuous because of the developing sporangia) 18

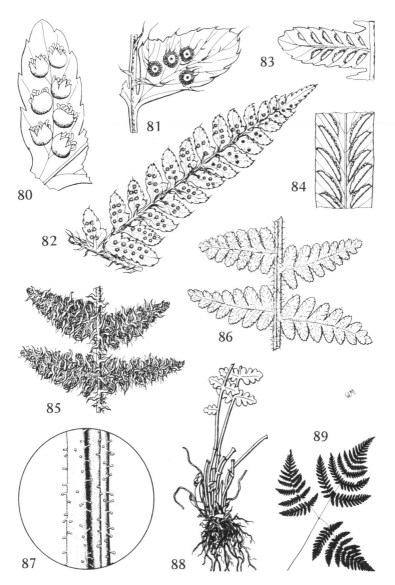

FIGURE 80. *Cystopteris fragilis*, fertile segment. FIGURE 81. *Polystichum Braunii* var. *Purshii*, fertile pinnule. FIGURE 82. *Polystichum Braunii* var. *Purshii*, fertile pinna. FIGURE 83. *Athyrium thelypterioides*, fertile segment. FIGURE 84. *Athyrium pycnocarpon*, portion of fertile pinna. FIGURE 85. *Woodsia ilvensis*, portion of leaf. FIGURE 86. *Woodsia scopulina*, portion of leaf. FIGURE 87. *Woodsia oregana*, portion of rachis (magnified). FIGURE 88. *Woodsia ilvensis*, basal portion of plant. FIGURE 89. *Gymnocarpium Dryopteris*, leaf.

18. Rachis and blade scaly, hairy or glandular (Figs. 85, 86, 87), or with a mixture
of scales, hairs, or glands 19

19. Rhizome long-creeping, the leaves
borne at intervals; pinnae, sometimes excepting the basal pair, attached to the rachis by green wings
or basal pinnae definitely the longest on the blade 20

20. Rachis and base of the mid-
nerves of the pinnae hairy . . . .
. . . . *Thelypteris* (p. 85)

20. Rachis and blade glabrous or
glandular . . . .
. . . . . *Gymnocarpium* (p. 89)

19. Rhizome compact, the leaves tufted;
pinnae not connected to the rachis
by green wings; the basal pinnae
definitely shorter than the longest
on the blade . . . . . *Woodsia* (p. 58)

18. Rachis and blade glabrous 21

21. Stipe jointed near its base (Fig. 88)
. . . . *Woodsia* (p. 58)

21. Stipe not jointed 22

22. Rachis shorter than or up to
the width of the blade; basal
pinnae much larger than the
second pair (Fig. 89); rhizome
long-creeping, the leaves borne
at intervals . . . . *Gymnocarpium Dryopteris* (p. 93)

22. Rachis usually at least twice as
long as the width of the blade;
basal pinnae rarely larger than
the second pair; leaves tufted;
rhizome usually compact . . . .
. . . . *Cystopteris* (p. 100)

Pteridium Gled. ex Scop.

Rhizome extensively creeping, deep-seated; blades bipinnate-pinnatifid to tripinnate-pinnatifid, the fertile similar to the sterile; veins free; sori consisting of a continuous marginal line, covered by a continuous marginal indusium.

Represented by a single species.

BRACKEN, *Pteridium aquilinum* (L.) Kuhn, Map 16, Fig. 90

The Bracken is one of our most distinctive ferns; its large, coarse, highly divided, usually ternate blade sets it apart from the others. The very young leaves make an acceptable vegetable similar to asparagus. They should be collected before the pinnae have unrolled and should be boiled a few minutes and served with butter or salt. They should be consumed in moderation, however, since Bracken contains principles that are deleterious when a regular part of the diet.

The Bracken grows in a variety of habitats—open areas or woods, damp or dry situations, rich humus or sandy soil. It prefers rather dry, open places and a light soil. It grows throughout the state except in some prairie areas.

Distribution: Our var. *latiusculum* (Desv.) Underw. occurs from Newfoundland to North Carolina, west to Wyoming and Oklahoma; also Mexico and Eurasia. Among the several varieties of this cosmopolitan species, var. *pubescens* is found in western North America and var. *pseudocaudatum* in the southern and southeastern United States.

Cryptogramma R. Br.

Rhizome creeping or compact and the fronds tufted; blades bipinnate to tripinnate, the fertile rather contracted and taller than the sterile; veins free; sori marginal, covered by a rather continuous marginal indusium.

SLENDER CLIFF BRAKE, *Cryptogramma Stelleri* (S. G. Gmel.) Prantl, Map 17, Fig. 91

This is a very delicate species, the sterile leaf being especially thin, the fertile more thickened and erect. The rhizome is unique among our ferns in that the portion bearing the leaves is plump and yellowish-green while the older portions are somewhat shriveled, brown, and hard.

90

FIGURE 90. *Pteridium aquilinum* var. *latiusculum*,
sterile blade 40 cm. long.

It grows in moist, shady places on calcareous rocks in the northeastern and southeastern parts of the state.

Distribution: Newfoundland to Alaska, south to West Virginia, Illinois, and Washington; Asia.

91

FIGURE 91. *Cryptogramma Stelleri*, leaves: *left*, sterile,
blade 6 cm. long; *right*, fertile, blade 6 cm. long.

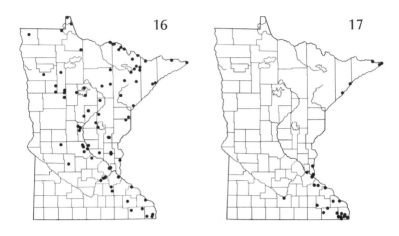

MAP 16. *Pteridium aquilinum* var. *latiusculum*.
MAP 17. *Cryptogramma Stelleri*.

PARSLEY FERN, *Cryptogramma crispa* (L.) R. Br.

This species grows on damp or dry cliffs on Isle Royale, Michigan, and there is a specimen in the University of Michigan Herbarium, collected by J. C. Jones (probably ca. 1865) from Farquhar Point, Minnesota. This locality has not been found, but a Farquhar Peak is near the

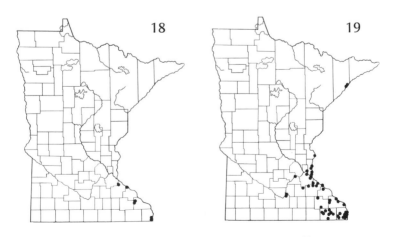

MAP 18. *Cheilanthes Feei*. MAP 19. *Pellaea glabella*.

Reservation River, Cook County. The species probably did grow in Minnesota, but an unequivocal record is required before it is definitely ascribed to the state.

The rhizome is rather stout, bearing tufted leaves which are thicker than those of *Cryptogramma Stelleri*. In North America *C. crispa* is represented by var. *acrostichoides* (R. Br.) C. B. Clarke; var. *crispa* is Eurasian.

Cheilanthes Sw.

Rhizome short-creeping or compact and the fronds tufted; blades bipinnate-pinnatifid to tripinnate, hairy, the fertile similar to the sterile; rachis dark brown to purple-brown; veins free; sori marginal, covered by a marginal indusium.

SLENDER LIP-FERN, *Cheilanthes Feei* Moore, Map 18, Fig. 92

This is a small, tufted species, with very hairy leaves. It is quite distinct, except perhaps from the Rusty Woodsia, but that species has scales as well as hairs on the leaf.

It grows on dry, exposed limestone cliffs. It is infrequent in the southeast part of the state.

Distribution: Wisconsin to British Columbia, south to Arkansas, Texas, and California.

HAIRY LIP-FERN, *Cheilanthes lanosa* (Michx.) D. C. Eaton [*Cheilanthes vestita* of Gray's Manual, ed. 8]

This species was collected a single time at the Dalles of the St. Croix River but without indication of the state, Minnesota or Wisconsin. It has not been rediscovered. It may be distinguished from the Slender Lip-fern by the hairy rather than smooth or only slightly hairy stipe and by the lanceolate-ovate ultimate segments rather than nearly round segments of *C. Feei*.

Distribution: Connecticut to Minnesota, south to Georgia and Texas.

Pellaea Link

Rhizome compact, the fronds tufted; blades pinnate to bipinnate, abruptly pinnate, the fertile similar to the sterile; rachis dark brown to purple-brown; veins free; sporangia borne on the vein ends, covered by a continuous marginal indusium.

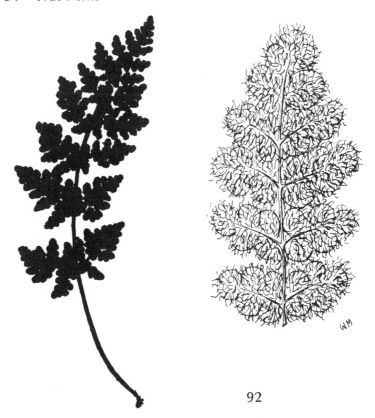

92

FIGURE 92. *Cheilanthes Feei*: *left*, fertile leaf, blade
6 cm. long; *right*, pinna.

KEY TO SPECIES

1. Rachis smooth or with a few scattered spreading hairs, reddish-brown
to dark brown, usually shining. . . . .*P. glabella* (p. 54)
1. Rachis definitely hairy with rather appressed hairs, dark purple-
brown, usually dull . . . . *P. atropurpurea* (p. 56)

SMOOTH CLIFF-BRAKE, *Pellaea glabella* Mett., Map 19, Fig. 93
[*Pellaea atropurpurea* var. *Bushii* Mackenzie]

The bluish-green, leathery, abruptly pinnate blade separates this
species from all except the next. From that, *P. atropurpurea*, it may be
separated by the characters in the key.

93

FIGURE 93. *Pellaea glabella*, fertile plants (many leaves removed), *right* blade 7 cm. long.

The Smooth Cliff-brake grows on limestone or unleached sandstone in damp or very dry exposed situations; it is rather common in the southeastern part of the state.

Distribution: Our var. *glabella* occurs from Quebec to South Dakota, south to Tennessee and Oklahoma; other varieties are in the western United States and adjacent Canada.

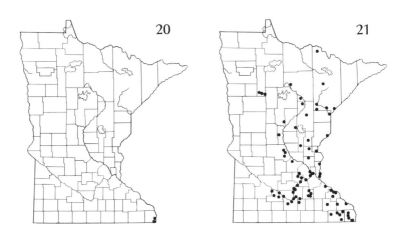

MAP 20. *Pellaea atropurpurea.* MAP 21. *Adiantum pedatum.*

PURPLE CLIFF-BRAKE, *Pellaea atropurpurea* (L.) Link, Map 20, Fig. 94

The dark pubescent rachis separates this species from the last. It is known from only three collections in Houston County, one made in 1899 at Jefferson, another in 1936, also from Jefferson and probably from the same place, and a third in 1949 near Brownsville. It grows on limestone cliffs.

Distribution: Vermont to British Columbia, south to Florida, Texas, and Mexico.

Adiantum L.

Rhizome creeping; blades bipinnate, the fertile and the sterile similar; stipe divided at its tip into two rachises, the pinnae arising from only one side of each rachis branch; stipe and rachis dark brown to purple-

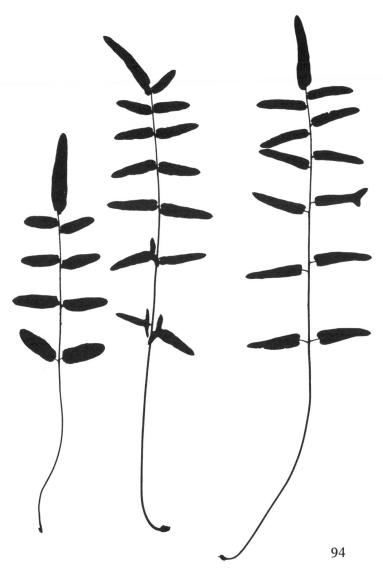

94

FIGURE 94. *Pellaea atropurpurea*, fertile leaves, *left*
blade 10 cm. long.

brown; veins free; sori marginal, covered by an elongate marginal indusium.

Represented in Minnesota by a single species.

MAIDENHAIR, *Adiantum pedatum* L., Map 21, Fig. 95

The Maidenhair is one of our most attractive species. It grows well under cultivation and makes nice borders in rich soil and shady places. The dark, shining stipe and rachis and the circular or semicircular blade are distinctive. Early in the year the stipe and rachis are usually glaucous. The rachis is branched to form two rachises, and the pinnae arise from only a single side of each rachis-branch.

The Maidenhair grows best in rich shaded leaf-mold, in woods, at the edges of swamps, on hillsides and in ravines in the central and southeastern parts of the state.

Distribution: The common Maidenhair is var. *pedatum*, from Quebec to Alaska, south to Georgia, Louisiana, and California; also in Asia. Var. *aleuticum* Rupr. grows especially on serpentine soils in eastern and in western North America.

Woodsia R. Br.

Rhizome compact, fronds tufted; blades pinnate to bipinnate-pinnatifid, the fertile similar to the sterile; veins free; sori roundish, more or less covered by the indusium which is attached below the sorus with the indusium segments curving over it.

KEY TO SPECIES

1. Stipe jointed near the base (Fig. 96); blade smooth, hairy, or scaly, not glandular; indusium of many thread-like segments (Fig. 97) . . .2
2. Blade hairy and scaly, usually copiously so, especially on the rachis and the lower surface, or if sparsely scaly, the scales at least on the distal veins and leaf tissue on the lower surface; pinnae oblong-tapering, the basal nearly or more than twice as long as broad . . . .*W. ilvensis* (p. 60)
2. Blade and rachis smooth or very sparingly hairy or scaly, or if scaly, the scales only in the midnerve and base of the main veins on the lower surface of the pinnae; pinnae round-ovate to triangular-ovate, the basal broader than long to only slightly longer than broad 3

FIGURE 95. *Adiantum pedatum*,
fertile leaf, blade 17 cm. long.

3. Stipe dark or reddish brown; rachis sparingly hairy or scaly,
   sometimes nearly smooth . . . . *W. alpina* (p. 62)
3. Stipe straw-colored or greenish; rachis smooth . . . .
   . . . . *W. glabella* (p. 62)
1. Stipe not jointed; blade glandular, sometimes also hairy; indusium of
   a few to several scale-like segments (as in Figs. 98, 99), only the tips
   sometimes thread-like 4
   4. Leaf glandular, not hairy 5
      5. Indusium of a few broad segments with short tips (Fig. 98);

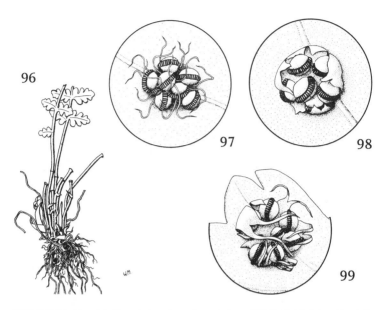

FIGURE 96. *Woodsia ilvensis,* basal portion of plant. FIGURE 97. *Woodsia alpina,* sorus (magnified). FIGURE 98. *Woodsia obtusa,* sorus (magnified). FIGURE 99. *Woodsia oregana* var. *Cathcartiana,* sorus (magnified).

    stipe entirely straw-colored, or light brown at the very base. . .

    . . . . *W. obtusa* (p. 63)

  5. Indusium of a few to several segments, these narrow or rather broad, with long thread-like tips (Fig. 99); stipes generally brown to dark brown or dark purple. . . . . *W. oregana* (p. 64)

  4. Leaf hairy with whitish flattened hairs, especially on the rachis and lower surface of the pinnae, also glandular . . . .

  . . . . *W. scopulina* (p. 64)

RUSTY WOODSIA, *Woodsia ilvensis* (L.) R. Br., Map 22, Fig. 100

This is our most common species and usually one of the most distinctive. The chaffy, hairy leaf is unlike any other, and as the leaf matures, the scales and hairs become a rusty brown color. Also the jointed stipe separates it from the other hairy species. Some forms are rather or quite smooth: these are mostly shade forms and may be separated from *W. alpina* by the cutting of the blade and the scales on the distal veins and leaf surface.

22

MAP 22. *Woodsia ilvensis.*

100    101

FIGURE 100. *Woodsia ilvensis*, fertile leaves, *left* blade 11 cm. long.
FIGURE 101. *Woodsia alpina*, fertile plants,
right blade 12 cm. long.

The Rusty Woodsia grows on a variety of rock types in damp, shady places or, more usually, in exposed crevices and on ledges. In suitable habitats it may be common or it may be infrequent.

Distribution: Greenland to Alaska, south to North Carolina, Iowa, and British Columbia; Eurasia.

ALPINE WOODSIA, *Woodsia alpina* (Bolton) S. F. Gray, Map 23, Fig. 101

The jointed stipe separates this species from all except *W. glabella* and *W. ilvensis.* It may be separated from *W. glabella* by the brown, usually reddish-brown, rather than straw-colored stipe, and usually by the presence of a few hairs and scales on the rachis. It may be separated from *W. ilvensis* by the cutting and the relative smoothness of the blade. The lower surface of the pinnae is smooth, or scaly only on the midnerve or at the base of the main veins.

It grows on calcareous rocks, usually in damp, shady places. It is rare in Lake and Cook counties.

Distribution: Greenland, south to New York, west to Minnesota.

SMOOTH WOODSIA, *Woodsia glabella* R. Br., Map 24, Fig. 102

This is a small delicate species, usually distinguished by its size and narrow blade. Large specimens are easily separated from *W. alpina* by the straw-colored or greenish stipe.

It grows on calcareous rocks, usually in deep shade in mossy, damp crevices but sometimes in more exposed places. It is rare in Lake and Cook counties.

Distribution: Newfoundland to Alaska, south to New York and British Columbia; Eurasia.

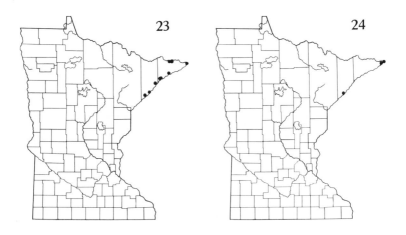

MAP 23. *Woodsia alpina.* Map 24. *Woodsia glabella.*

FIGURE 102. *Woodsia glabella*, fertile plants, *lower center* blade 4.5
cm. long. FIGURE 103. *Woodsia obtusa*, fertile
leaves, *right* blade 20 cm. long.

BLUNT-LOBED WOODSIA, *Woodsia obtusa* (Spreng.) Torr., Map 25,
Fig. 103

The indusium with a few rather large, scale-like segments that are
pointed or blunt at the tip is characteristic of this species. *W. oregana*,
which occurs in the same range, has long thread-like tips on the indusial
segments and usually a brown stipe, while the stipe of *W. obtusa* is
straw-colored or light brown only at the very base.

It grows on acidic or basic rocks in either shady or rather sunny situa-

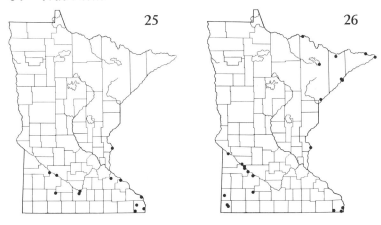

MAP 25. *Woodsia obtusa.* MAP 26. *Woodsia oregana.*

tions. One collection was made in sandy soil at the base of a cliff. It is found in the southern part of the state.

Distribution: Maine to Minnesota, south to Florida and Texas.

OREGON WOODSIA, *Woodsia oregana* D. C. Eaton, Map 26, Fig. 104 [*Woodsia Cathcartiana* Robinson, *Woodsia oregana* var. *Cathcartiana* (Robins.) Morton]

The long, thread-like tips of the indusial segments separate this species from *W. obtusa*; from *W. scopulina* it may be separated by the lack of the whitish flattened hairs so characteristic of that species. It is glandular and usually has a brown to dark purple stipe. Late in the season the leaves may be only slightly glandular.

It grows on various types of rocks either in damp, shady places or in exposed situations, in the southwest part of the state, in the southeast corner, and in the eastern and northeastern sections.

Distribution: Quebec to California and British Columbia.

ROCKY-MOUNTAIN WOODSIA, *Woodsia scopulina* D. C. Eaton, Map 27, Fig. 105

This species is easily distinguished by the whitish, flattened hairs of the leaf. It is also glandular; the glands are usually, but not always, yellowish.

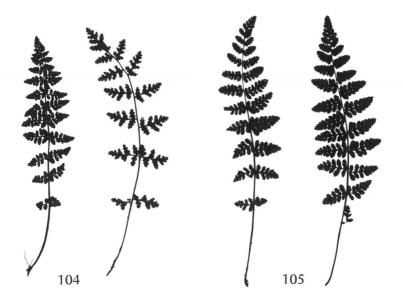

FIGURE 104. *Woodsia oregana*, fertile leaves (two types), *left* blade
10 cm. long. FIGURE 105. *Woodsia scopulina*, fertile leaves,
left blade 11 cm. long.

It grows in Cook County on calcareous rocks in rather damp, shaded situations or sometimes in more open places.

Distribution: Quebec to Alaska and California.

HYBRIDS

Woodsia alpina X *ilvensis*, Map 28. [*Woodsia ilvensis* var. *gracilis* Lawson, *Woodsia* X *gracilis* (Lawson) Butters]

This hybrid is intermediate in its characters between the two parent species, in the chaffiness and hairiness of the blade and in the cutting of the blade. Some specimens are rather close to *W. alpina* and others rather close to *W. ilvensis*; most are quite intermediate. The sporangia are mostly abortive, but a few do mature and the spores from these are probably viable. The abortive sporangia is the best distinguishing feature for those specimens that are close in other characters to either of the parent species.

It has been collected in crevices and ledges of slate cliffs or basic igneous rock in the company of both parents in Lake and Cook counties.

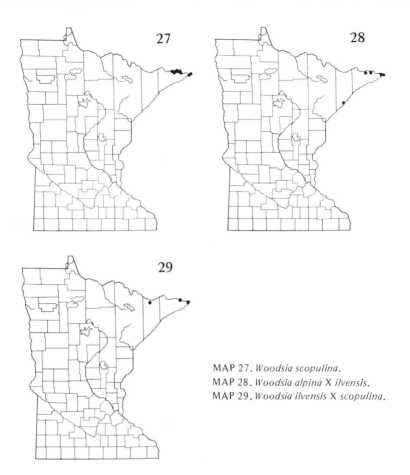

MAP 27. *Woodsia scopulina.*
MAP 28. *Woodsia alpina* X *ilvensis.*
MAP 29. *Woodsia ilvensis* X *scopulina.*

Woodsia ilvensis X *scopulina*, Map 29. [*Woodsia* X *Abbeae* Butters]

This hybrid is scaly, like *W. ilvensis*, but the scales are not abundant and it has the whitish, flattened hairs of *W. scopulina*. Immature leaves show the indument best; old leaves usually have few hairs and scales. It is glandular, and the sporangia are all abortive.

It has been collected on calcareous cliffs at three localities in Cook and Lake counties.

Matteuccia Todaro

Rhizome large, often erect, stoloniferous; blades pinnate-pinnatifid, the fertile greatly contracted with the pinnules inrolled toward the midvein of the pinna and soon turning brown, the sterile expanded and green; veins free; sori becoming contiguous, indusium early-deciduous.

Represented in Minnesota by a single species.

OSTRICH FERN, *Matteuccia Struthiopteris* (L.) Todaro, Map 30, Figs. 106, 107 [*Pteretis pensylvanica* (Willd.) Fern.

In the Ostrich Fern, like the Sensitive Fern, the fertile leaf is completely different from the sterile; the segments of the pinnae are inrolled to enclose the sporangia, giving the pinnae a tubelike appearance. It is brown at maturity and much shorter than the sterile leaf.

The sterile blade is characteristic, having the lower pinnae gradually reduced until the lowest ones are very small; the tip of the blade is rather abrupt. Stolons are usually present on the rootstock, and the plant spreads by this means, often forming large colonies.

Most of the Minnesota specimens are finely pubescent, especially on the front of the rachis; this gradually wears off as the season progresses. An extreme phase with more or less persistent hairs on the sides and back as well as on the front of the rachis is frequent in the state and grades imperceptibly into the smooth phase. Another phase, sometimes occurring in the state, has the upper basal pinnules on many of the pinnae elongate and curved part way around the rachis.

The young leaves may be prepared as a vegetable in the spring. They should be collected when a few inches tall and cooked like asparagus.

The Ostrich Fern grows in moist or wet places, most typically in stream or river alluvium or sand deposits; also in swampy woods, in

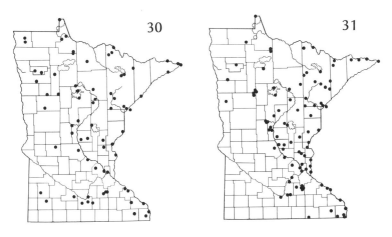

MAP 30. *Matteuccia Struthiopteris* var. *pensylvanica*.
MAP 31. *Onoclea sensibilis*.

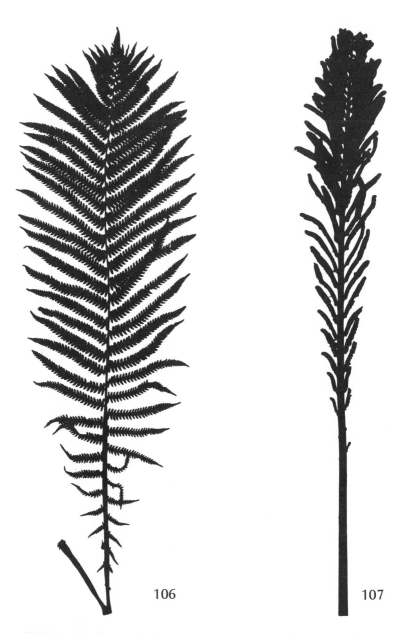

106

107

FIGURE 106. *Matteuccia Struthiopteris* var. *pensylvanica*, sterile leaf, blade
65 cm. long. FIGURE 107. *Matteuccia Struthiopteris* var.
pensylvanica, fertile leaf, blade 18 cm. long.

108

FIGURE 108. *Onoclea sensibilis*: *left*, sterile leaf, blade 18 cm.
long; *right*, fertile leaf, blade 9 cm. long.

thickets, and on rich, shady, moist hillsides. It grows throughout the state except in the prairie areas.

Distribution: In North America is var. *pensylvanica* (Willd.) Morton, from Newfoundland to Alaska, south to Virginia, Missouri, and British Columbia. Var. *Struthiopteris* is Eurasian.

Onoclea L.

Rhizome relatively large, extensively creeping; fertile blade contracted, bipinnate, veins free, pinnules inrolled, soon becoming brown; sterile blade deeply pinnatifid to pinnate-pinnatifid, expanded and green, veins forming a network; sori roundish, covered by an early-deciduous indusium.

Represented in Minnesota by a single species.

SENSITIVE FERN, *Onoclea sensibilis* L., Map 31, Fig. 108

The coarse cutting of the blade and the veins that form a network easily separate this species from the others. The rhizome is long-creeping, and the fertile leaf is quite different from the sterile. It is compact; the pinnules are inrolled and rather ball-like, enclosing the sporangia; and it is brown when mature.

A form that is intermediate between the fertile and sterile leaves, f. *obtusilobata* (Schkuhr) Gilbert, may be found in the state.

The Sensitive Fern grows best in moist or wet places, in woods, thickets, or open marshes, and fruits best in sunny situations. It grows throughout the state except in the west central and southwestern parts.

Distribution: Newfoundland south to Florida, west to South Dakota and Texas; eastern Asia.

Polystichum Roth

Rhizome relatively large, compact; blades pinnate or bipinnate, the fertile similar to the sterile, the segment margins bristly toothed; sori round, covered by a round indusium attached at the center.

BRAUN'S HOLLY FERN, *Polystichum Braunii* (Spenner) Fée, Map 32, Figs. 82, 109

This is a distinctive species. The leaves are bipinnate, dark green, glossy above and scaly beneath. The stipe and rachis are heavily chaffy with light brown scales.

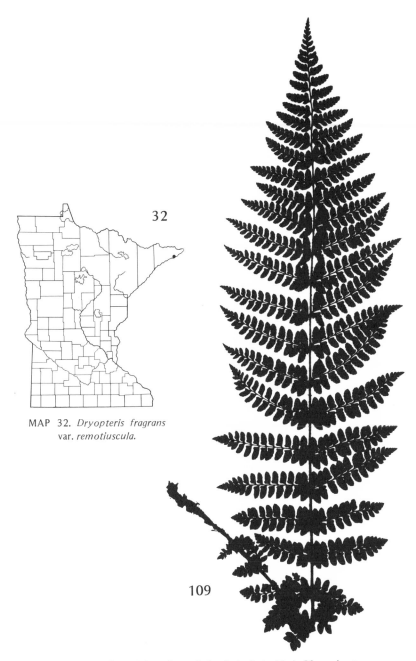

MAP 32. *Dryopteris fragrans*
var. *remotiuscula.*

109

FIGURE 109. *Polystichum Braunii*: fertile leaf, the blade 50 cm. long.

It has only recently been discovered in a gorge of the Kodonce River, Cook County, where it grows in fissures and on small ledges of a basic lava rock.

Distribution: The eastern North American variety is var. *Purshii* Fern., from Newfoundland to Minnesota, and south to New England, New York, and the mountains of Pennsylvania; var. *Braunii* is Eurasian and Alaskan.

Another species, *Polystichum Lonchitis* (L.) Roth has been collected at Cloud Bay, Thunder Bay District, Ontario and should be searched for on calcareous rocks in adjacent Cook County. The blade is once-pinnate (Fig. 71), and the fertile pinnae are similar to the sterile ones.

Polystichum acrostichoides (Michx.) Schott, with a once-pinnate blade and apical, somewhat contracted, fertile pinnae, previously known from Allamakee County, Iowa, was recently discovered in Minnesota. It was found on east- and north-facing river bluffs, growing in mixed hardwood forests, Houston and Winona counties.

Dryopteris Adans.

Rhizome relatively large, compact or short-creeping; stipes scaly; rachis not hairy; blades bipinnate to tripinnate-pinnatifid, the fertile similar to the sterile or slightly contracted and more erect; veins free; sori round, covered by a heart-shaped indusium attached at its sinus.

KEY TO SPECIES

1. Margins of the segments smooth, or if toothed, the teeth blunt (Figs. 110, 111) 2
    2. Rachis not glandular, often somewhat scaly; blade not glandular, rather broad (Fig. 112); sori marginal; indusium about one-fourth or one-fifth as broad as the segment upon which it is borne . . . . .
    . . . .*D. marginalis* (p. 73)
    2. Rachis glandular and scaly; blade glandular, rather narrow (Fig. 113); sori borne about halfway between the margin and the midnerve; indusia very large, from half as broad as to broader than the segments upon which they are borne. . . . .
    . . . . *D. fragrans* (p. 74)
1. Segments toothed and the teeth pointed (Fig. 114) 3
    3. Blade pinnate-pinnatifid to bipinnate-pinnatifid; the basal pinnules on the basal pinnae sessile. 4
    4. Lower basal pinnules on the basal pinnae definitely shorter

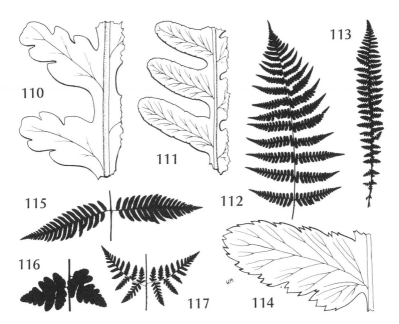

FIGURE 110. *Dryopteris fragrans* var. *remotiuscula*, portion of pinna. FIGURE 111. *Dryopteris marginalis*, portion of pinna. FIGURE 112. *Dryopteris marginalis*, leaf 27 cm. long. FIGURE 113. *Dryopteris fragrans* var. *remotiuscula*, leaf. FIGURE 114. *Dryopteris spinulosa*, pinnule. FIGURE 115. *Dryopteris Goldiana*, basal pinnae. FIGURE 116. *Dryopteris cristata*, basal pinnae. FIGURE 117. *Dryopteris spinulosa*, basal pinnae.

than the longest on the pinnae (Fig. 115); blade relatively broad; sori borne near the midnerve of the segment . . . .
. . . . *D. Goldiana* (p. 74)

4. Lower basal pinnules on the basal pinnae the longest or almost the longest on the pinnae (Fig. 116); blade relatively narrow; sori borne about halfway between the margin and the midnerve of the segment . . . .*D. cristata* (p. 77)

3. Blade bipinnate-pinnatifid to tripinnate; the basal pinnules on the basal pinnae stalked (Fig. 117). . . . . *D. spinulosa* (p. 77)

MARGINAL SHIELD-FERN, *Dryopteris marginalis* (L.) A. Gray, Fig. 112

This species is not known to grow in Minnesota but is known from adjacent areas: Isle Royale, Michigan; Grant County, Wisconsin; and

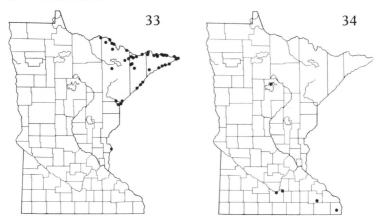

MAP 33. *Dryopteris fragrans* var. *remotiuscula*. MAP
34. *Dryopteris Goldiana*.

Allamakee County, Iowa. It should be sought on rocky hillsides in the
southeastern and northeastern parts of the state. The leathery-textured
leaves and the marginal sori are distinguishing features.

FRAGRANT FERN, *Dryopteris fragrans* (L.) Schott, Map 33, Fig. 118

The Fragrant Fern is characterized by its glandular blade which is
somewhat fragrant, its very large indusia, and the persistence of leaves
of previous years on the rhizome. It grows in crevices or on ledges of
various types of rocks, acidic or basic, and in dry and sunny or shady
situations.

It is confined to the northeastern part of the state with the exception
of the station at Taylor's Falls.

Distribution: Our var. *remotiuscula* Komarov is distributed from
Labrador to Ontario, south to New York and Minnesota; var. *fragrans*
is northern, Greenland to Alaska; and Eurasia.

GOLDIE'S FERN, *Dryopteris Goldiana* (Hook.) A. Gray, Map 34,
Fig. 119

Goldie's Fern is very rare in Minnesota, being known from only four
localities. Only one of our collections has been made since 1899. The
large, relatively broad leaves with sessile and shallowly toothed pinnules
are distinctive, as are also the sori that are borne near the midnerve of
the segments. It grows in rich, deciduous woods in the southern and

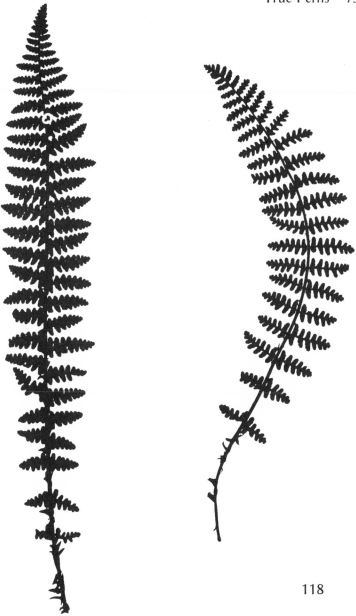

118

FIGURE 118. *Dryopteris fragrans* var. *remotiuscula*, fertile
leaves, *left* blade 16 cm. long.

119

FIGURE 119. *Dryopteris Goldiana*, fertile leaf, blade 30 cm. long.

southeastern parts of the state and in Ottertail Point, Leech Lake, in Cass County.
Distribution: New Brunswick to Minnesota, south to South Carolina and Iowa.

CRESTED FERN, *Dryopteris cristata* (L.) A. Gray, Map 35, Fig. 120

The fertile leaves of the Crested Fern are especially characteristic; they are taller and more erect than the sterile and are relatively long and narrow. The shape of the blade and the sessile pinnules distinguish it from *D. spinulosa*.

The Crested Fern grows in a variety of habitats, especially where the soil is rich and moisture is abundant. Alder thickets, wet, deciduous woods, and coniferous swamps or bogs are favorite habitats; rarely it may grow in sandy soil or even on a sandstone ledge. It is distributed in the central and northeastern parts of the state; there is one station in the southeastern corner.

Distribution: Newfoundland to Alberta, south to Louisiana, Nebraska, and Idaho.

SPINULOSE SHIELD-FERN, *Dryopteris spinulosa* (O. F. Müll.) Watt [*Dryopteris austriaca* (Jacq.) Woynar]

The Spinulose Shield-fern may be separated from the other species of *Dryopteris* by its bristly toothed segments, the stalked pinnules, at least the basal ones on the basal pinnae, and the generally lacy cutting of the leaves. It grows in a variety of damp, shady habitats.

35

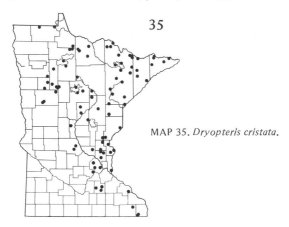

MAP 35. *Dryopteris cristata.*

120

FIGURE 120. *Dryopteris cristata: left,* sterile leaf, blade 17 cm. long; *right,* fertile leaf, blade 32 cm. long.

It is represented in Minnesota by three strongly marked varieties that are treated by some authors as separate species. Their natural variation sometimes makes identification uncertain, and they may, accordingly, be treated as varieties of a complex species.

KEY TO VARIETIES

1. Indusium and the blade not glandular; lower basal pinnules on the basal pinnae longer than the adjacent ones 2
    2. Lower basal pinnules on the basal pinnae usually closer to the upper basal pinnules than to the second upper ones (Fig. 121), only rarely closer to the second ones or more than 4 mm. from the basal ones; most of the terminal teeth on the pinnules or pinnule-segments longer than broad; most of the lateral teeth on the ultimate segments incurved (Fig. 122) . . . .
    . . . .*D. spinulosa* var. *spinulosa* (p. 79)
    2. Lower basal pinnules on the basal pinnae usually closer to the second upper pinnules than to the upper basal ones (Fig. 123), at least 5 mm. distant from the upper basal ones; most of the terminal teeth on the pinnules as broad as long or broader than long; many of the lateral teeth on the ultimate segments divergent (excepting the bristle-tip) (Fig. 124) . . . .
    . . . . *D. spinulosa* var. *americana* (p. 82)
1. Indusium and often the blade glandular (Figs. 125, 126), especially on the rachis and at the base of the pinnae; lower basal pinnules on the basal pinnae shorter than the adjacent ones (Fig. 127). . . . .
    . . . . *D. spinulosa* var. *intermedia* (p. 82)

Dryopteris spinulosa var. *spinulosa*, Map 36, Fig. 128 [*Dryopteris austriaca* var. *spinulosa* (O. F. Müll.) Fiori]

The typical variety of the Spinulose Shield-fern is distinguished by having the lower basal pinnules on the basal pinnae longer than the adjacent ones and close to the upper basal pinnules. The incurved teeth on the ultimate segments also distinguish it from var. *americana*.

It grows in swamps, bogs, or swampy woods and in other damp or wet habitats, sometimes on rocky hillsides or even cliffs, rarely in sandy soil, throughout the state, but it is rare in the prairie areas.

Distribution: Quebec to British Columbia, south to Kentucky and Missouri; Eurasia.

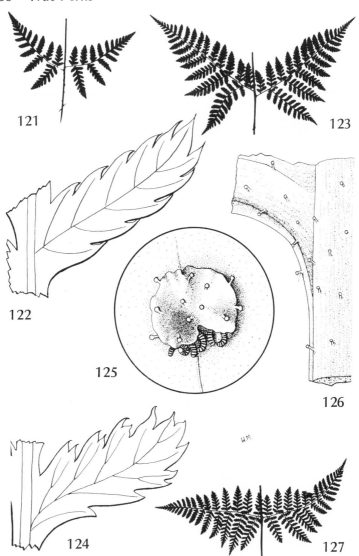

FIGURE 121. *Dryopteris spinulosa* var. *spinulosa*, basal pinnae. FIGURE 122. *Dryopteris spinulosa* var. *spinulosa*, segment. FIGURE 123. *Dryopteris spinulosa* var. *americana*, basal pinnae. FIGURE 124. *Dryopteris spinulosa* var. *americana*, segment. FIGURE 125. *Dryopteris spinulosa* var. *intermedia*, sorus (magnified). FIGURE 126. *Dryopteris spinulosa* var. *intermedia*, portion of rachis and base of pinna (magnified). FIGURE 127. *Dryopteris spinulosa* var. *intermedia*, basal pinnae.

128

FIGURE 128. *Dryopteris spinulosa* var. *spinulosa*,
fertile leaf, blade 30 cm. long.

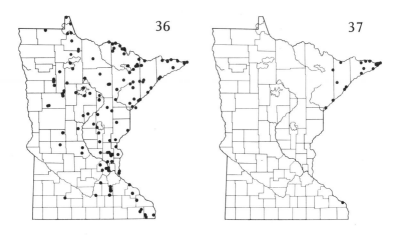

MAP 36. *Dryopteris spinulosa* var. *spinulosa*. MAP 37.
Dryopteris spinulosa var. *americana*.

Dryopteris spinulosa var. *americana* (Fisch.) Fern., Map 37, Fig. 129
[*Dryopteris austriaca* (Jacq.) Woynar var. *austriaca*]

This variety has a relatively broad blade that is highly divided and the ultimate segments have most of the lateral teeth divergent so as to give a lacy appearance to the blade. The lower basal pinnules are usually closer to the second upper ones than to the basal upper pinnules. It has been found growing in moist, rich, coniferous or deciduous woods, or on hillsides in Lake, Cook, and St. Louis counties; there is a single record of occurrence south in Winona County.

Distribution: Greenland to Alaska, south to North Carolina, Minnesota, and Washington.

Dryopteris spinulosa var. *intermedia* (Muhl.) Underw., Map 38, Fig. 130
[*Dryopteris austriaca* var. *intermedia* (Muhl.) Morton]

This variety is well marked by its glandular indusium and usually glandular blade. The lower basal pinnules on the basal pinnae are shorter than the adjacent ones, and the blade has a lacy appearance.

Var. *intermedia* grows in moist, rich, coniferous or deciduous woods or on rocky slopes in the northeastern and southeastern parts of the state.

Distribution: Newfoundland to Minnesota, south to Georgia and Iowa.

129

FIGURE 129. *Dryopteris spinulosa* var. *americana*,
fertile blade 35 cm. long.

130

FIGURE 130. *Dryopteris spinulosa* var. *intermedia*, fertile leaf, blade 35 cm. long.

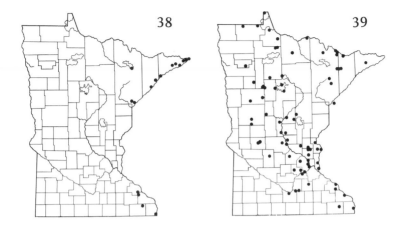

MAP 38. *Dryopteris spinulosa* var. *intermedia*. MAP 39. *Thelypteris palustris* var. *pubescens*.

HYBRIDS

Hybrids are known between many of the species and varieties of *Dryopteris*. Few of them have been reported from Minnesota, probably because not many of the species commonly grow together. Careful search, however, will undoubtedly increase the number known and the georgraphic records of them.

Dryopteris cristata X *spinulosa* var. *intermedia* [*Dryopteris* X *Boottii* (Tuckerm.) Underw.]. Becker County. The leaf outline is very similar to that in the next (cf. Fig. 131) but the blade and indusia are glandular.

Dryopteris cristata X *spinulosa* var. *spinulosa* Fig. 131. [*Dryopteris* X *uliginosa* (Döll) Druce] Kanabec and Itasca Counties. The blade and indusia are glabrous.

Dryopteris spinulosa var. *intermedia* X var. *spinulosa* [*Dryopteris* X *triploidea* Wherry; *Dryopteris spinulosa* var. *fructuosa* (Gilbert) Trudell]. Roseau County. The blade of this hybrid is similar in appearance to that of var. *intermedia*, but it is somewhat more coarsely cut. The abortive spores provide the most certain means of identification.

Thelypteris Schmidel

Rhizome slender, extensively creeping; stipe scarcely or not at all scaly; rachis hairy; blades pinnate-pinnatifid to bipinnate-pinnatifid, the

131

FIGURE 131. *Dryopteris cristata* X *spinulosa* var. *spinulosa*,
fertile blade, 35 cm. long.

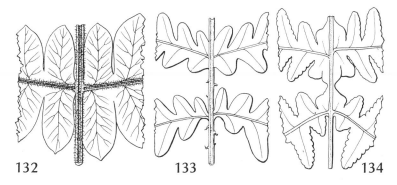

132   133   134

FIGURE 132. *Thelypteris palustris* var. *pubescens*, base of pinnae. FIGURE
133. *Thelypteris Phegopteris*, base of the basal and second pair of pinnae.
FIGURE 134. *Thelypteris hexagonoptera*, base of the basal
and second pair of pinnae.

fertile similar to the sterile or slightly contracted and more erect; veins
free; sori round, covered by a heart-shaped indusium attached at its
sinus or indusium absent.

KEY TO SPECIES

1. Pinnae essentially sessile but not connected to the rachis by green
   wings (Fig. 132); width of the blade not more than half the length
   of the rachis; indusium present, withering at the maturity of the
   sporangia . . . . *T. palustris* (p. 89)
1. Pinnae above the basal pair connected to the rachis by broad green
   wings (Fig. 133); width of the blade usually nearly equal to or
   slightly exceeding the length of the rachis; indusium absent 2
   2. Basal pinnae sessile but not connected to the rachis by green
      wings (Figure 133) (rarely the upper basal pinnule-segment par-
      tially fused to the rachis), completely separate from the second
      pair of pinnae; longest pinnule-segments on the basal pinnae entire
      or rarely shallowly lobed . . . . *T. Phegopteris* (p. 89)
   2. Basal pinnae connected to the rachis on the upper side by green
      wings, these connecting the rachis with the base of the pinna or
      with the upper basal pinnule-segment (Fig. 134), usually also con-
      necting with the wings of the second pair of pinnae; longest
      pinnule-segment on the basal pinnae pinnatifid . . . .
      . . . . *T. hexagonoptera* (p. 89)

135

FIGURE 135. *Thelypteris palustris* var. *pubescens*, plants with sterile
leaves (several leaves removed), *right* blade 18 cm. long.

Large stand of Ostrich Fern, *Matteuccia Struthiopteris*,
growing in low, wet woods.

Planting of Lady Fern, *Athyrium Filix-femina*,
with other herbs, in rustic setting.

Fertile stem of Wood Horsetail,
Equisetum sylvaticum, as seen
at the edges of bogs
in northern Minnesota.

Round-branched Ground-pine,
Lycopodium dendroideum, a frequent
inhabitant of the forests
of northern Minnesota.

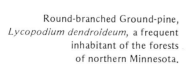

Ground Cedar, *Lycopodium complanatum,* most characteristic
of upland coniferous forests of the state.

Middle section of spore-bearing leaf of Interrupted Fern, *Osmunda Claytoniana*. This fern is often seen in large colonies in moist woods.

top and bottom:
Rattlesnake Fern,
Botrychium virginianum,
found in most
habitats throughout
the wooded parts
of the state.

Facing page. Fiddlehead of Interrupted Fern, *Osmunda Claytoniana*. As in most ferns, the young leaves are coiled during the early stages of growth.

Crested Fern, *Dryopteris cristata*, shown in association
with Sphagnum Moss, in a sunny bog.

acing page. Cinnamon Fern, *Osmunda cinnamomea.* The brown leaves
ear the spores; the green leaves are photosynthetic.
his fern grows best in very wet places.

Oak Fern, *Gymnocarpium Dryopteris*. This delicate plant
is often seen in moist woods of the coniferous zone.

Smooth Cliff-brake, *Pellaea glabella*. Abundant in crevices
of limestone ledges in southeastern Minnesota.

MARSH FERN, *Thelypteris palustris* Schott, Map 39, Fig. 135 [*Dryopteris Thelypteris* (L.) A. Gray var. *pubescens* (Lawson) Nakai]

The Marsh Fern is distinguished by its generally lanceolate blade, pinnatifid pinnae, and creeping rhizome. The fertile blade is usually somewhat contracted, the fertile pinnules having a revolute margin, and it is more erect than the sterile. It grows in marshes and swamps, at the edge of lakes and in other wet habitats, and reaches its best development in sunny rather than in shady habitats. The Marsh Fern is common in the central part of the state.

Distribution: The northern and eastern var. *pubescens* (Lawson) Fernald occurs from Newfoundland to Manitoba, south to Georgia and Oklahoma; other varieties grow in the southern United States, the West Indies, South Africa, Eurasia, and New Zealand.

LONG BEECH-FERN, *Thelypteris Phegopteris* (L.) Slosson, Map 40, Fig. 136 [*Dryopteris Phegopteris* (L.) C. Chr.]

The Long Beech-fern may be distinguished from the related Broad Beech-fern by the basal pinnae that are not connected to the rachis by wings. It is a rather common species in humus in coniferous or deciduous woods or thickets and is often found on ledges or in crevices of cliffs in the northeastern part of the state; there are also a few records of its occurrence in the southeastern corner of the state.

Distribution: Greenland to Alaska, south to North Carolina, Iowa, and Oregon.

BROAD BEECH-FERN, *Thelypteris hexagonoptera* (Michx.) Weath., Map 41, Fig. 137 [*Dryopteris hexagonoptera* (Michx.) C. Chr.]

The broadly triangular blade of the Broad Beech-fern and the completely winged rachis separate it from the other species of the genus.

The only collections have been made in Houston and Fillmore counties. Its habitat is the damp, north-facing river bluffs, in mixed hardwood forests.

Distribution: Quebec to Minnesota, south to Florida and Texas.

Gymnocarpium Newm.

Rhizome slender, extensively creeping; neither stipe nor rachis scaly or hairy; blades bipinnate-pinnatifid, the fertile similar to the sterile; veins free; sori round, indusium absent.

136

FIGURE 136. *Thelypteris Phegopteris: left,* fertile plant (with several leaves removed), blade 16 cm. long; *right,* fertile leaf.

137

FIGURE 137. *Thelypteris hexagonoptera*, fertile leaf,
blade 22 cm. long.

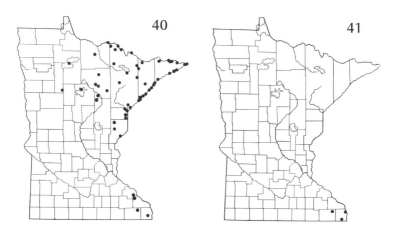

MAP 40. *Thelypteris Phegopteris.* MAP 41. *Thelypteris hexagonoptera.*

KEY TO SPECIES

1. Rachis smooth or rarely slightly glandular; blade ternate, each basal pinnae approximating the size of the central segment, it broadly triangular with an acute tip (Fig. 138) . . . . *G. Dryopteris* (p. 93)
1. Rachis glandular (Fig. 139); blade long-triangular, not ternate; each basal pinna definitely smaller than the central segment, it long-triangular with a tapering tip (Fig. 140) . . . . *G. Robertianum* (p. 93)

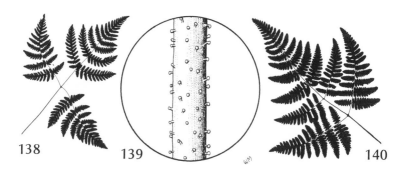

138   139   140

FIGURE 138. *Gymnocarpium Dryopteris,* leaf. FIGURE 139. *Gymnocarpium Robertianum,* portion of rachis (magnified). FIGURE 140. *Gymnocarpium Robertianum,* leaf.

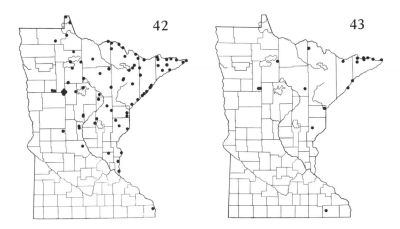

MAP 42. *Gymnocarpium Dryopteris.* MAP 43.
Gymnocarpium Robertianum.

OAK FERN, *Gymnocarpium Dryopteris* (L.) Newm., Map 42, Fig. 141
[*Dryopteris disjuncta* (Ledeb.) Morton]

The Oak Fern is characterized by its small ternate blade. It is closely related to *G. Robertianum,* from which it may be separated by the shape and relative size of the basal pinnae and the central segment. In the Oak Fern the basal pinnae are broadly triangular, and each is almost as large as the broadly triangular central segment. The Northern Oak Fern has the basal pinnae long-triangular and definitely smaller than the central segment, which is long-triangular with a tapering tip. Also it is quite glandular on the rachis; the Oak Fern is usually glabrous, but rarely a phase with a slightly glandular rachis occurs.

It grows in rich, moist woods and occasionally on boulders or cliffs in the north-central and northeastern parts of the state.

Distribution: Greenland to Alaska, south to Virginia, Iowa, and Arizona; Eurasia.

NORTHERN OAK-FERN, *Gymnocarpium Robertianum* (Hoffm.) Newm., Map 43, Fig. 142 [*Dryopteris Robertiana* (Hoffm.) C. Chr.]

The differences between this species and the closely related Oak Fern are discussed under that species.

The Northern Oak-fern grows in coniferous woods or especially on

141

FIGURE 141. *Gymnocarpium Dryopteris*, portion of fertile plant
(several leaves removed), blade 12 cm. long.

142

FIGURE 142. *Gymnocarpium Robertianum*, fertile blade 13 cm. long.

calcareous cliffs. A single collection from Cook County is from a granite cliff which might well be acidic. It is infrequent in Lake and Cook counties and rare southward.
Distribution: Newfoundland to Alaska, south to Pennsylvania, Iowa and British Columbia.

HYBRID

Gymnocarpium Dryopteris X *Robertianum* [*Gymnocarpium* X *heterosporum* Wagner]

This putative hybrid, which is intermediate between the parental species in most of its characters, has been reported from Carlton, Lake, and St. Louis counties. The spores are of various sizes, rather than of a nearly uniform size as in the species, and this characteristic provides the most certain means of identification.

Athyrium Roth

Rhizome creeping, relatively large; blades pinnate to tripinnate, large, the fertile similar to the sterile but usually slightly contracted and more erect; veins free; sori elongate, straight, hooked or occasionally horseshoe-shaped, covered by an indusium attached along one side.

KEY TO SPECIES

1. Blade once-pinnate, the pinnae entire or slightly toothed . . . .
. . . .*A. pycnocarpon* (p. 96)
1. Blade pinnate-pinnatifid or more highly divided 2
2. Blade pinnate-pinnatifid; pinnule segments usually entire; rachis and midnerves of the pinnae usually with narrow scales; sori mostly straight . . . . *A. thelypterioides* (p. 99)
2. Blade usually bipinnate or more highly divided; the pinnule-segments or pinnules lobed or deeply toothed; rachis and mid-nerves of the pinnae smooth; sori mostly curved . . . .
. . . . *A. Filix-femina* (p. 99)

NARROW-LEAVED SPLEENWORT, *Athyrium pycnocarpon* (Spreng.) Tidestr., Map 44, Fig. 143

This species is easily distinguished by its once pinnate blade. The sterile leaves are very thin for so large a fern. The fertile leaves are more erect than the sterile, and the pinnae narrower.

143

FIGURE 143. *Athyrium pycnocarpon: left*, sterile blade
40 cm. long; *right*, tip of fertile blade.

144

FIGURE 144. *Athyrium thelypterioides*,
fertile blade 55 cm. long.

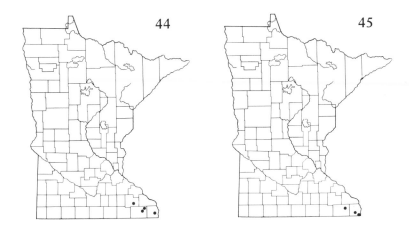

MAP 44. *Athyrium pycnocarpon*. MAP 45. *Athyrium thelypterioides.*

It grows in rich humus on shady hillsides only in the extreme southeast corner of the state.

Distribution: Quebec to Minnesota, south to Georgia and Louisiana.

SILVERY SPLEENWORT, *Athyrium thelypterioides* (Michx.) Desv., Map 45, Figure 144

The stipe, rachis, and midnerves of the pinnae are usually finely chaffy. The blade is pinnate-pinnatifid, the pinnae are long tapering at the tip, and the pinnule-segments are entire or shallowly toothed. A phase with the pinnule-segments more or less coarsely toothed is f. *acrostichoides* (Sw.) Gilbert.

The Silvery Spleenwort grows on rich, damp, shady slopes only in the extreme southeast corner of the state.

Distribution: Nova Scotia to Minnesota, south to Georgia and Louisiana; eastern Asia.

LADY FERN, *Athyrium Filix-femina* (L.) Roth, Map 46, Figs. 145-149 [*Athyrium angustum* (Willd.) Presl]

The Lady Fern has a superficial resemblance to some of the species of *Dryopteris*, from which it may be separated by the lack of any hairs or scales on the blade and the rounded or acutely pointed teeth without a bristle tip. It is an excellent species for the garden, thriving under a variety of conditions.

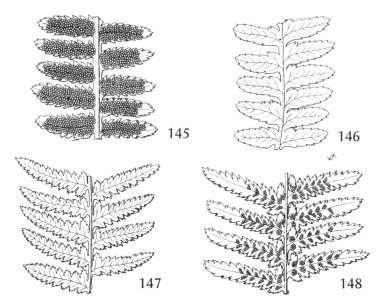

FIGURES 145-148. *Athryium Filix-femina*, portions of pinnae showing variation. FIGURE 145. Fertile. FIGURE 146. Sterile. FIGURE 147. Sterile. FIGURE 148. Fertile.

It grows in open places, in thickets or woods, swamps or bogs, and occasionally in crevices of rocks or on ledges. It is absent only from the southwestern and northwestern parts of the state.

Distribution: Our northeastern var. *Michauxii* (Spreng.) Farwell occurs from Quebec to South Dakota, south to Tennessee and Missouri; other varieties grow in the southern United States, in western North America, and in Eurasia.

Cystopteris Bernh.

Rhizome creeping, compact or elongate; blades bipinnate to bipinnate-pinnatifid, the fertile similar to the sterile; veins free; sori roundish, covered by a cup-shaped indusium that is attached at its base and arches over the sporangia.

KEY TO SPECIES

1. Blade broadest above the base; most of the veins ending in a tooth . .
. . . . *C. fragilis* (p. 102)

149

FIGURE 149. *Athyrium Filix-femina* var. *Michauxii*.
fertile leaf, blade 35 cm. long.

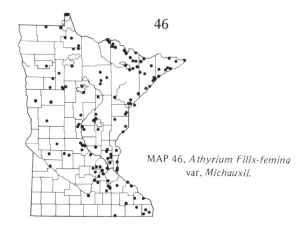

MAP 46. *Athyrium Filix-femina*
var. *Michauxii.*

1. Blade broadest at the base; most of the veins ending in a notch
   (sinus). . . . .*C. bulbifera* (p. 106)

FRAGILE FERN, *Cystopteris fragilis* (L.) Bernh. [*Cystopteris Dickeana*
Sim]

   The Fragile Fern is one of the commonest species. It is quite variable
in leaf and may easily be mistaken for a *Woodsia,* but the lack of hairs,
scales, or glands on the leaf will separate it from any Woodsias that are
similar.

   Cystopteris fragilis is a complex species and its variations are not
adequately understood. The three major, sometimes intergrading, types
in Minnesota are recognized as varieties.

KEY TO VARIETIES*

1. Rhizome short, or if elongate, thickly beset with the stipe-bases of
   the old leaves, the growing point not elongate beyond the leaves of
   the season; basal pinnule-segments sessile or nearly so (as in Fig. 151)
  2
   2. Indusium rather large, up to 1 mm. long, more or less cleft at the
      apex (Fig. 150); basal pinnule-segments broadened at the base
      (Fig. 151), not evenly wedge-shaped . . . .
      . . . . *C. fragilis* var. *fragilis* (p. 103)

*Adapted from Weatherby, *Rhodora* 37:375, 1935.

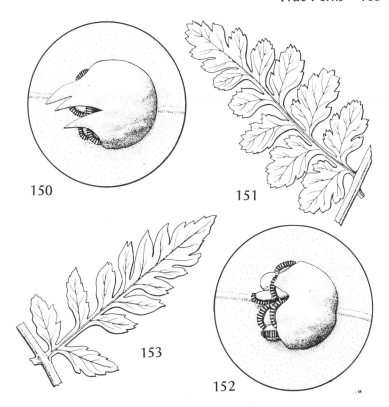

FIGURE 150. *Cystopteris fragilis* var. *fragilis*, sorus. FIGURE 151. *Cystopteris fragilis* var. *fragilis*, pinna. FIGURE 152. *Cystopteris fragilis* var. *Mackayi*, sorus. FIGURE 153. *Cystopteris fragilis* var. *Mackayi*, pinna.

2. Indusium about 0.5 mm. long, entire or only shallowly cleft (Fig. 152); basal pinnule-segments evenly wedge-shaped at the base (Fig. 153) . . . . *C. fragilis* var. *Mackayi* (p. 104)
1. Rhizome long-creeping, the growing point produced well beyond the leaves of the season (2 cm. or more); basal pinnules definitely stalked (Fig. 156); indusium about 0.5 mm. long, entire or shallowly cleft . . . . *C. fragilis* var. *protrusa* (p. 104)

C. fragilis var. *fragilis*, Map 47, Fig. 154

The typical variety has the basal pinnule-segments broad at the base and sessile or nearly so; the indusium is rather long and deeply cleft.

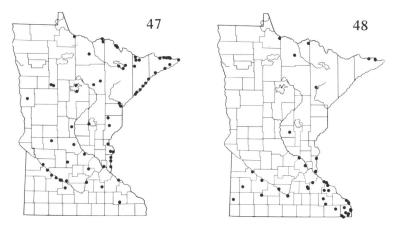

MAP 47. *Cystopteris fragilis* var. *fragilis*. MAP 48.
Cytopteris fragilis var. *Mackayi*.

It grows on a variety of types of rocks in damp, shaded, or sunny exposed situations, sometimes in soil. This variety is common except in
the northwestern and west-central parts of the state.
   Distribution: Labrador to Alaska, south to North Carolina and California; Eurasia.

C. fragilis var. *Mackayi* Lawson, Map 48, Fig. 155

   This variety has a short, entire indusium and has the basal pinnule-
segments evenly wedge-shaped at the base.
   On or near various types of rocks, usually in shaded places. This
variety is found predominantly in the southern part of the state and is
rare northward.
   Distribution: Nova Scotia to North Dakota, south to Virginia and
Missouri.

C. fragilis var. *protrusa* Weatherby, Map 49, Fig. 156

   This is the best marked of the varities. It has a long-creeping rootstock with the growing point prolonged beyond the leaves of the year,
and the basal pinnules are definitely stalked.
   It grows, not on rocks, but in rich, damp, shady woods in the southeast corner of the state.
   Distribution: New York to Minnesota, south to Georgia and Oklahoma.

154

155

156

FIGURE 154. *Cystopteris fragilis* var. *fragilis*, fertile leaf, blade 20 cm. long.
FIGURE 155. *Cystopteris fragilis* var. *Mackayi: left*, sterile leaf, blade 7 cm.
long; *right*, fertile leaf, blade 12 cm. long. FIGURE 156. *Cystopteris fragilis*
var. *protrusa*, fertile plant (several leaves removed), blade 14 cm. long.

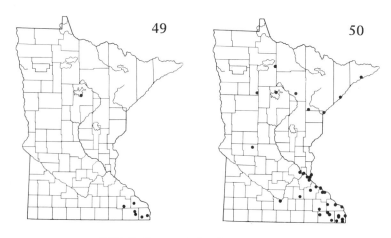

MAP 49. *Cystopteris fragilis* var. *protrusa.*
MAP 50. *Cystopteris bulbifera.*

BULBET FERN, *Cystopteris bulbifera* (L.) Bernh., Map 50, Fig. 157

The large leaves are long-tapering and bear bulblets. Small leaves may be confused with *C. fragilis* but may be distinguished by the characters mentioned in the key. The bulblets drop from the leaves and will grow and produce new plants under favorable conditions. The long leaves are most attractive and make this one of the best species for the rock garden providing a sufficiently damp and shady place is available.

It grows most commonly on damp, shady calcareous rocks but occasionally on rocky banks or in woods, particularly in the southeastern part of the state.

Distribution: Newfoundland to Utah, south to Georgia and Arizona.

HYBRID

Cystopteris bulbifera X *fragilis* var. *fragilis* Map 51, Fig. 158. [*Cystopteris* X *laurentiana* (Weatherby) Blasdell, *Cystopteris fragilis* var. *laurentiana* Weatherby].

This hybrid is similar to *C. fragilis* var. *fragilis*, but the leaf is usually larger. The minutely glandular indusium serves to identify it.

Asplenium L.

Rhizome small, compact, fronds tufted; blades once pinnate, the fertile and sterile similar, stipe and rachis dark brown to purple-brown;

157

FIGURE 157. *Cystopteris bulbifera*, fertile leaves,
right blade 27 cm. long.

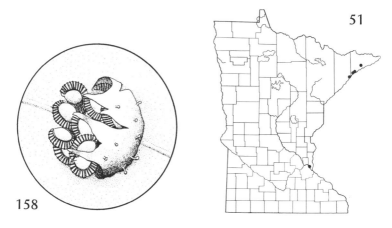

FIGURE 158. *Cystopteris bulbifera* X *fragilis* var *fragilis*. MAP 51.
Cystopteris bulbifera X *fragilis* var. *fragilis*.

veins free; sori elongate, covered by an indusium attached along one side.
A single species in Minnesota.

MAIDENHAIR SPLEENWORT, *Asplenium Trichomanes* L., Map 52, Figure 159

The tufted leaves, which are long and narrow and once-pinnate with a dark stipe and rachis, make this a distinctive species. It is one of our rare ones, however, growing on cliffs, ledges, or crevices in parts of Cook County and in one, now unknown locality, in Goodhue County.
Distribution: Quebec to Alaska, south to Georgia, Arizona, and Oregon; Eurasia.

Asplenium platyneuron (L.) D. C. Eaton was recently discovered in the southeastern corner of the state, in Fillmore, Houston, and Winona counties. It was known earlier from Allamakee County, Iowa, just south of Houston County and was to be expected in Minnesota. It grows on east- and north-facing river bluffs in mixed hardwood forests.

Camptosorus Link

Rhizome small, compact; blades entire, the margin entire or somewhat irregular, the fertile similar to the sterile but more often with an

159

FIGURE 159. *Asplenium Trichomanes*, fertile plant, longest
leaf 17 cm. long.

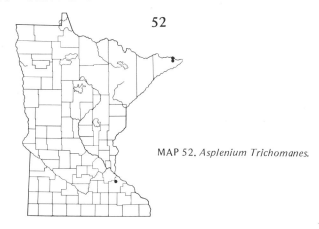

MAP 52. *Asplenium Trichomanes.*

elongate tip; veins forming a network; sori irregular, mostly elongate and straight, covered by an indusium attached along one side.

Represented in Minnesota by a single species.

WALKING FERN, *Camptosorus rhizophyllus* (L.) Link, Map 53, Fig. 160

The Walking Fern is one of our most unusual species; in favorable habitats the tip of the leaf takes root in the moss or soil and a new plant

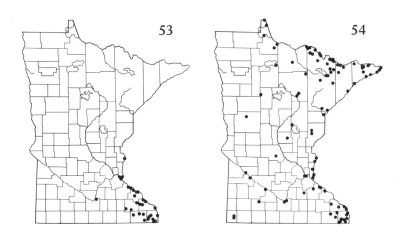

MAP 53. *Camptosorus rhizophyllus.* MAP 54. *Polypodium virginianum.*

160

FIGURE 160. *Camptosorus rhizophyllus*, plants, long leaves
fertile, short leaves sterile, longest leaf 15 cm. long.

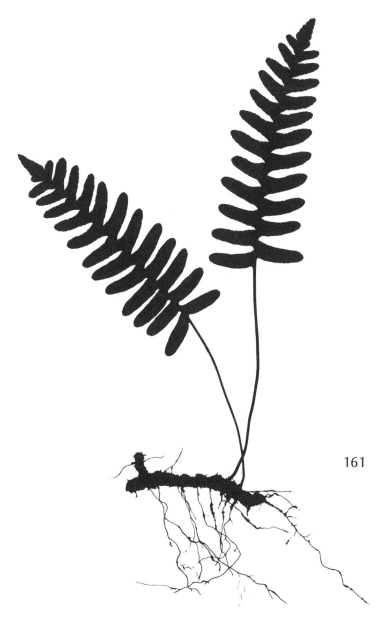

161

FIGURE 161. *Polypodium virginianum*, fertile plant, *right*
blade 10 cm. long.

arises. Sometimes three "generations" may be found, all connected to the same plant. The unusual-shaped leaf and the veins that form a network are distinctive. A form with the basal lobes of the blades of the larger leaves of the plant greatly prolonged, f. *auriculatus* R. Hoffm., is known from two localities.

The Walking Fern grows in damp, shady situations on calcareous rocks in the southeastern part of the state.

Distribution: Quebec to Minnesota, south to Georgia and Oklahoma.

Polypodium L.

Rhizome elongate, the older parts bearing scars of the leaf-bases; blades deeply pinnatifid, the fertile similar to the sterile; veins free; sori round, indusium absent.

Represented in Minnesota by a single species.

COMMON POLYPODY, *Polypodium virginianum* L., Map 54, Fig. 161 [*Polypodium vulgare* var. *virginianum* (L.) Eaton]

The blade of the Common Polypody is deeply pinnatifid, but not quite pinnate. It is evergreen and of a leathery texture. The rhizome bears the scars of the old leaves, which break off cleanly.

The Common Polypody grows on a great variety of rock types, usually in a rather shady place but sometimes in the sun. Rarely it will grow on the bank of a sandy ravine. It grows throughout the state in suitable habitats.

Distribution: Newfoundland to British Columbia, south to Georgia and Arkansas.

Fern Allies

HORSETAIL FAMILY, Equisetaceae

Aerial stems erect from a deep, branched rhizome, mostly hollow, with an external silicon deposit, longitudinally grooved, jointed at the conspicuous nodes; branches and leaves borne in whorls at the nodes, the leaves much reduced to form sheaths; sporangia borne on specialized leaves in a terminal cone; spores of one kind. (Glossary Plate 3, p. 117) Represented in Minnesota by a single genus.

Equisetum L.

Many species have branched and unbranched phases and various types of branches, erect or decumbent, simple or compound, and so forth. These forms have not been recognized, being generally considered to be ecological phases, several sometimes being found on the same plant. For a detailed discussion of the American forms of *Equisetum* see Victorin, Les Equisetinées du Quebec, Contrib. Lab. Bot. Univ. Montréal, No. 9, 1927. R. L. Hauke, in the *Transactions of the Wisconsin Academy of Science, Arts and Letters*, vol. 54, has presented a modern revision of the genus for Wisconsin, which is followed here.

KEY TO SPECIES

1. Stems fertile, brownish except that occasionally the sheaths may be green, or very small green branches may be present 2
   2. Teeth of the sheaths with a white margin; stem becoming branched with green branches . . . . *E. pratense* (p. 127)
   2. Teeth of the sheaths brown to blackish in color 3

114

3. Stem becoming branched with green branches; teeth of the sheaths coherent in a few groups, reddish brown, the groups with rounded to broadly acute tips. . . .*E. sylvaticum* (p. 129)

3. Stem not branched, soon withering; teeth of the lower sheaths dark brown to blackish, mostly separate, with long acuminate tips. . . . .*E. arvense* (p. 129)

1. Stems fertile or sterile, green 4

4. Stems rather curly and twisted, lacking a central hollow* (Fig. 162), but with three small hollows outside the center, with six ridges; sheaths with three teeth . . . . *E. scirpoides* (p. 123)

4. Stem usually straight, with a central hollow,* usually with more than six ridges; sheaths of the main stem with more than three teeth. 5

5. Central hollow very large in relation to the diameter of the stem, the stem wall thin; small outermost hollows (Fig. 163) opposite the ridges of the stem, that is, on the same radius . . . .*E. fluviatile* (p. 123)

5. Central hollow large or small, stem wall usually relatively thick; outermost small hollows alternate with the stem ridges, that is, on a different radius (a third set of smaller hollows often between the central one and the outermost, as in Fig. 164). . . .6

6. Stem not branched above the base or only irregularly so and the branches ascending .7

7. Sheaths gray, sometimes with one or two black bands, or the lower sheaths darker; teeth of the sheaths usually soon falling; stem rough with silica deposit; cones apiculate . . . . *E. hyemale* (p. 116)

7. Sheaths, at least the upper ones, green or pale green, rarely gray only at the base of the teeth; lower sheaths sometimes gray 8

8. Teeth of the sheaths soon falling, sometimes a few on a sheath persistent. . . . .*E. laevigatum* (p. 119)

8. Teeth of the sheaths persistent (Fig. 165) . . . .
. . . . E. variegatum (p. 119)

6. Stems branched above the base in a regular manner, the branches often spreading 9

* To observe the internal structure, cross sections should be taken from about the middle of an internode in about the middle of the stem.

9. Teeth on the sheaths of the main stem reddish brown, coherent in a few groups, especially toward the base of the stem (Fig. 166); branches branched; spicules of silica usually present on the main stem .*E. sylvaticum* (p. 129)

9. Teeth of the sheaths on the main stem whitish to black, sometimes brown but not reddish brown, separate or coherent in pairs, branches only rarely branched 10

10. Central hollow of the main stem about the same size as the outermost hollows (Fig. 167); sheaths on the first internode of the branches with five or more teeth. . . . . *E. palustre* (p. 125)

10. Central hollow of the main stem usually definitely larger than the outermost hollows (Fig. 164); sheaths on the first internodes of the branches with three or four teeth (as in Fig. 168). 11

11. Ridges of the main stem with spicules of silica deposit, especially on the upper part of the upper internodes; first internodes of the branches at the first-branched node shorter than the sheath and the teeth at that node (Fig. 168) . . . . *E. pratense* (p. 127)

11. Ridges of the main stem usually roughened but lacking spicules of silica deposit; first internode of the branches at the first-branched node usually longer than the sheath and teeth at that node (Fig. 169). . . . . *E. arvense* (p. 129)

TALL SCOURING-RUSH, *Equisetum hyemale* L., Map 55, Fig. 170 [*Equisetum hyemale* var. *pseudohyemale* (Farwell) Morton]

The rough, unbranched stem with ashy-gray sheaths and the deciduous teeth distinguish this species from our others. Rarely it has some erect branches.

It grows along stream or river banks, on lake shores, and in other moist habitats, and also in dry, open places, prairies, road cuts, and dry woods almost throughout the state.

Distribution: Our representative is var. *affine* (Engelm.) A. A. Eaton, widely distributed in North America, Quebec to Alaska and south to Guatemala; also in eastern Asia. Var. *hyemale* is Eurasian.

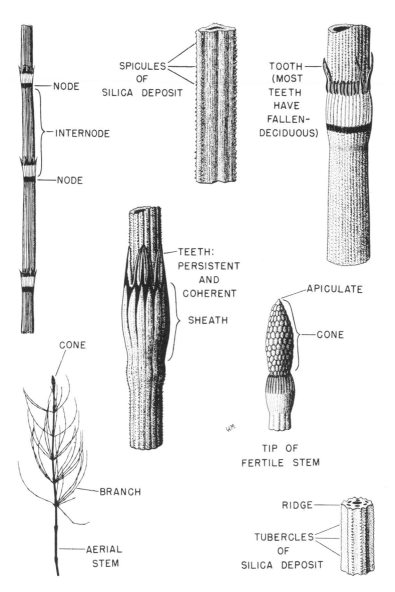

SPICULES
OF
SILICA DEPOSIT

NODE

INTERNODE

NODE

TOOTH
(MOST
TEETH
HAVE
FALLEN-
DECIDUOUS)

TEETH:
PERSISTENT
AND
COHERENT

SHEATH

APICULATE

CONE

CONE

TIP OF
FERTILE STEM

BRANCH

AERIAL
STEM

RIDGE

TUBERCLES
OF
SILICA DEPOSIT

GLOSSARY PLATE 3. Illustrations of special terms used to describe the
characteristic features of the Horsetail Family.

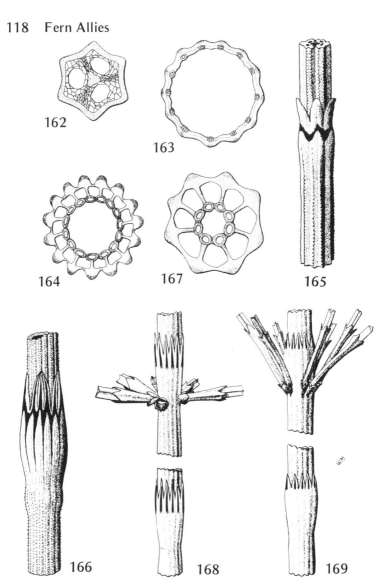

FIGURE 162. *Equisetum scirpoides*, section of stem (magnified). FIGURE 163. *Equisetum fluviatile*, section of stem (magnified). FIGURE 164. *Equisetum arvense*, section of stem (magnified). FIGURE 165. *Equisetum variegatum*, portion of stem. FIGURE 166. *Equisetum sylvaticum*, portion of stem. FIGURE 167. *Equisetum palustre*, section of stem (magnified). FIGURE 168. *Equisetum pratense*, portion of stem and bases of branches. FIGURE 169. *Equisetum arvense*, portion of stem and bases of branches.

SMOOTH SCOURING-RUSH, *Equisetum laevigatum* A. Br. Map 56, Fig. 171 (habit similar to that of *E. hyemale*) [*Equisetum hyemale* var. *intermedium* A. A. Eaton, *Equisetum kansanum* Schaffner]

The green sheaths, at least the upper ones, and smoother stem separate this from *E. hyemale* and the unbranched stem and deciduous teeth separate it from the other species. Rarely the stem may have a few erect branches.

It grows in moist or dry places, often in sandy soil—prairies, river banks, lake shores, beaches, or meadows in all but the northern part of the state.

Distribution: Ontario to British Columbia, south to Ohio, Texas, and northern Mexico.

VARIEGATED SCOURING-RUSH, *Equisetum variegatum* Schleich., Map 57, Fig. 172

This species can be distinguished from the other unbranched ones by its persistent teeth and two-angled ridges with two rows of tubercles. The stem is rather small and slender; the green sheaths often turn blackish with age.

It grows in wet places or in shallow water, on lake shores and stream banks, in swampy ground and in ditches. It is rare in the northern part of the state.

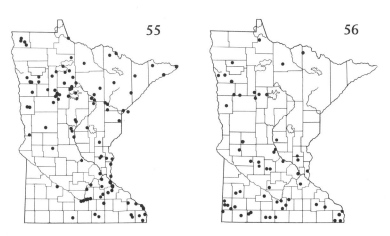

MAP 55. *Equisetum hyemale* var. *affine*. MAP 56.
Equisetum laevigatum.

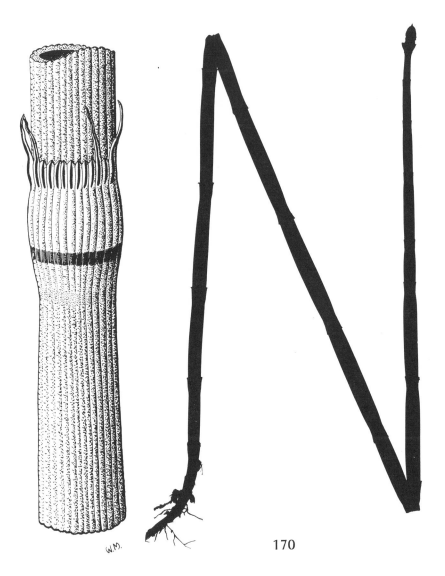

170

FIGURE 170. *Equisetum hyemale* var. *affine*: *left*, portion
of stem (enlarged); *right*, fertile stem 85 cm. long.

171

FIGURE 171. *Equisetum laevigatum*, tip of fertile stem (enlarged).

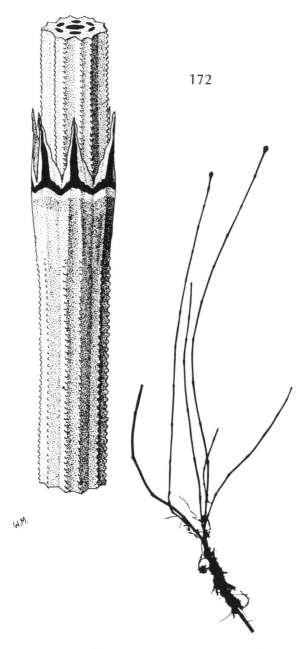

FIGURE 172. *Equisetum variegatum: left*, portion of stem
(enlarged); *right*, fertile plant 30 cm. tall.

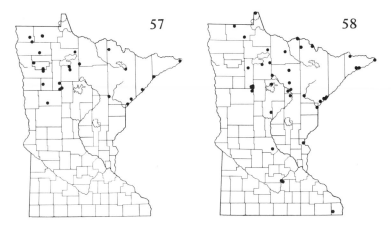

MAP 57. *Equisetum variegatum*. MAP 58. *Equisetum scirpoides*.

Distribution: Greenland to Alaska, south to Pennsylvania, Minnesota, Colorado, and California; Eurasia.

DWARF SCOURING-RUSH, *Equisetum scirpoides* Michx., Map 58, Fig. 173

The small, curly stems with six ridges and three teeth on the sheaths make this species one of our most distinctive. Also it is our only species that does not have a central hollow in the stem, although there are three hollows between the center and the stem wall.

It grows in low woods, coniferous swamps, and other moist shady places. The collection from Houston County is from calcareous ledges. The Dwarf Scouring-rush is scattered throughout most of the state but is absent from the prairie regions.

Distribution: Greenland to Alaska, south to New York, Montana, and Washington; Eurasia.

WATER HORSETAIL, *Equisetum fluviatile* L., Map 59, Fig. 174

The Water Horsetail is characterized by a large central hollow and a thin stem wall. There are usually from fifteen to twenty or more teeth on the sheaths. The small outer hollows are opposite the stem ridges. Some plants are entire, unbranched; others have a few ascending branches; and some have many spreading branches at each node.

It grows in bogs or swamps in a variety of soils, most characteristically

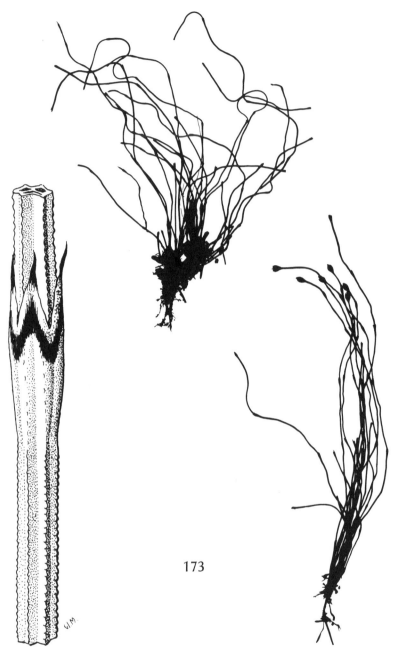

173

FIGURE 173. *Equisetum scirpoides: left,* portion of stem (enlarged);
upper, sterile plant; *right,* fertile plant 15 cm. tall.

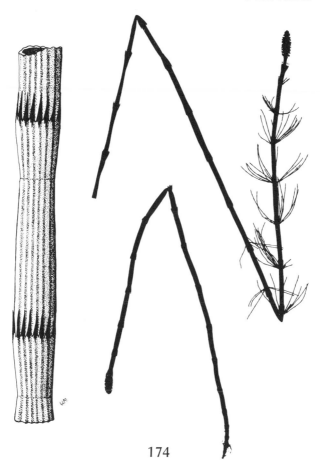

174

FIGURE 174. *Equisetum fluviatile: left*, portion of stem (enlarged); *right*, fertile stems, the upper 50 cm. long.

in lakes, streams, or ditches in water from a few inches to about three feet deep. It is rather generally distributed throughout the state.

Distribution: Newfoundland to Alaska, south to Pennsylvania, Minnesota, and Oregon; Eurasia.

MARSH HORSETAIL, *Equisetum palustre* L., Map 60, Fig. 175

The small central hollow of the stem and the sheaths of the branches with five or more teeth separate this species from the other branched

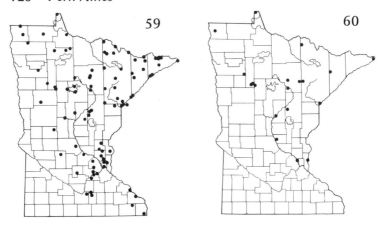

MAP 59. *Equisetum fluviatile.* MAP 60. *Equisetum palustre.*

ones. There is a strong tendency for the sheaths to flare outward and then narrow at their mouth. The type of branching varies considerably.

It grows in swamps or ditches or in open, wet places such as lake shores or springy areas in the central and northeastern parts of the state.

Distribution: Quebec to Alaska, south to Pennsylvania, Nebraska, and California; Eurasia.

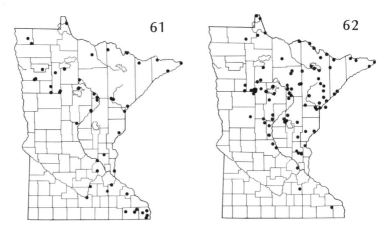

MAP 61. *Equisetum pratense.* MAP 62. *Equisetum sylvaticum* var. *sylvaticum* and intermediates with var. *pauciramosum.*

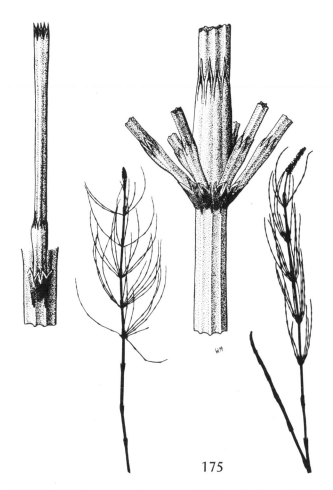

175

FIGURE 175. *Equisetum palustre: upper left,* branch of stem (enlarged);
upper center, portion of stem and bases of branches (enlarged);
lower, fertile stems, the right one 50 cm. tall.

MEADOW HORSETAIL, *Equisetum pratense* Ehrh., Map 61, Fig. 176

This species and the next, *E. sylvaticum,* are the only two that have
spicules of silica deposit on the stem; in the others the silica deposit is
smooth or in the form of dots or tubercles. It may be distinguished from
E. sylvaticum by the simple rather than compound branches. The teeth
on the sheaths are separate and have a white border. It is also charac-

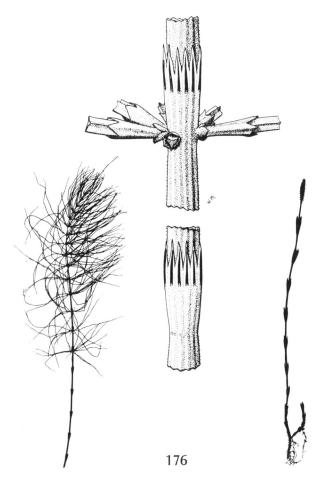

176

FIGURE 176. *Equisetum pratense: center,* portion of stem and
bases of branches (enlarged); *lower left,* sterile stem;
lower right, fertile stem 30 cm. tall.

terized by the first internode of the branches being shorter than the
sheath at that node, especially at the lowest branch-bearing nodes. The
fertile stems are, at first, quite different from the sterile, being unbranched and brownish; but soon green branches are produced, and
after the cone withers and the branches are fully developed, it is like
the sterile.

The Meadow Horsetail grows in woods and occasionally in rather open places in the eastern and northwestern parts of the state.

Distribution: Newfoundland to Alaska, south to New Jersey, Iowa, and British Columbia; Eurasia.

WOOD HORSETAIL, *Equisetum sylvaticum* L., Map 62, Fig. 177

The relatively large, reddish-brown teeth, coherent in a few groups, are characteristic of the Wood Horsetail. Also the branches are again branched, and the stem usually has spicules of silica deposit. The fertile shoots are unlike the sterile, at first being unbranched and brownish, but green branches are soon produced, and when the cone withers they appear like the sterile. Two phases are found in the state, one (Fig. 177D), with short spicules, and the other with the branches smooth (Fig. 177E), and numerous intermediates occur between them.

This species grows in woods, usually those that are moist and rather shady; occasionally it will grow in more open habitats.

Distribution: Labrador to Alaska, south to Maryland, Nebraska, and Oregon; Eurasia.

FIELD HORSETAIL, *Equisetum arvense* L., Map 63, Fig. 178

As a species this is one of our most distinctive, being the only one that has the fertile stems completely brownish and withering at the maturity of the cone. *E. pratense* and *E. sylvaticum* have brownish stems at first, but they soon become green and branched with green branches.

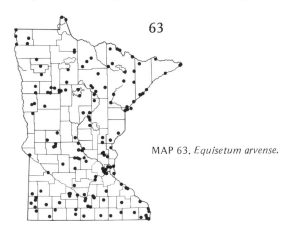

63

MAP 63. *Equisetum arvense.*

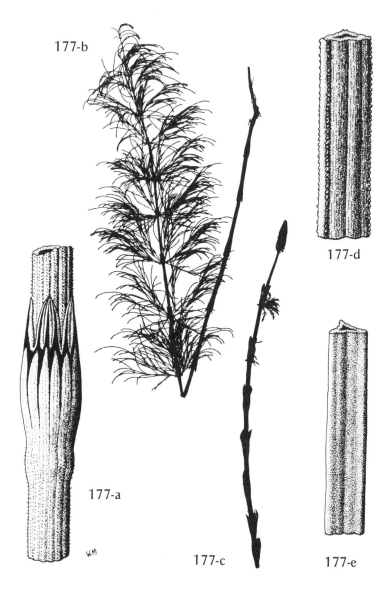

FIGURE 177. *Equisetum sylvaticum*: 177A, portion of stem (enlarged); 177B, sterile stem 50 cm. tall; 177C, fertile stem 30 cm. tall; 177D, portion of first internode of branch (enlarged); 177E, portion of first internode of a branch (enlarged).

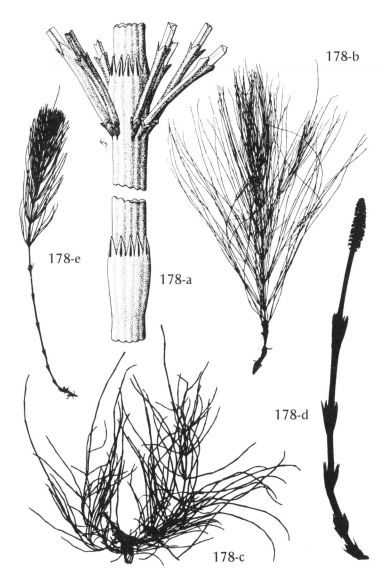

FIGURE 178. *Equisetum arvense*: 178A, portion of stem and bases of branches (enlarged); 178B, sterile stem 35 cm. tall; 178C, sterile stem 15 cm. tall; 178D, fertile stem 15 cm. tall; 178E, sterile stem 30 cm. tall.

The sterile stems of *E. arvense* are not at all distinctive, however, and can be best separated from the species they resemble as follows: from *E. pratense* by the spicules of silica of that species, from *E. sylvaticum* by the reddish-brown teeth on the sheaths of that species, and from *E. palustre* by the small central hollow of that species.

E. arvense has the primary branches four-angled and the sheaths with four teeth or has them with three angles and the sheaths with three teeth. It varies considerably in its mode of branching, as illustrated in Figs. 178B, C and E.

The Field Horsetail grows throughout the state in prairies, along railroad embankments, and in other open places. It will grow either in dry or in moist soil, and usually the soil will be rather sterile. Only occasionally will it be found growing in woods or thickets. Locally it is often of some importance as a soil binder.

Distribution: The Field Horsetail is widespread in the United States and Canada; Eurasia.

HYBRIDS

Four hybrids of Equisetum species have been recognized in Minnesota. Since these are technically difficult to distinguish from the parental species, they have not been included in the key.

Equisetum arvense X *Equisetum fluviatile* [*Equisetum* X *litorale* Kuehl.]

A single record is known from Washington County. The hybrid closely resembles *E. fluviatile* but has small outer hollows in the stem that are alternate with the stem ridges.

Equisetum hyemale var. *affine* X *Equisetum laevigatum* [*Equisetum* X *Ferrissii* Clute]

This hybrid is evidently rather widespread through the state. Its characters are quite intermediate between those of the parents.

Equisetum hyemale var. *affine* X *Equisetum variegatum* [*Equisetum* X *trachyodon* A. Braun]

A few specimens have been collected in the northern part of the state. The hybrid is similar to *E. variegatum* but the teeth of the sheaths have very slender tips.

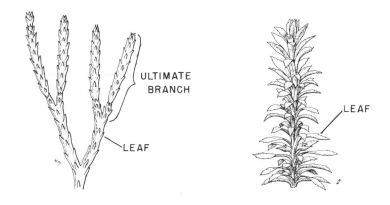

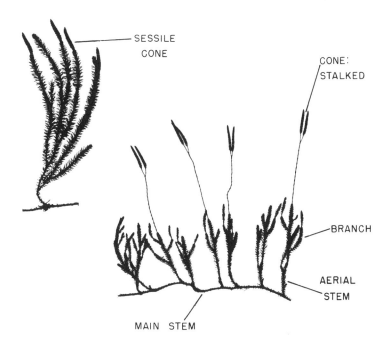

GLOSSARY PLATE 4. Illustrations of some of the terms that are used when describing members of the Club Moss Family.

Equisetum laevigatum X *Equisetum variegatum* [*Equisetum* X *Nelsonii*
(A. A. Eaton) Schaffner, *Equisetum variegatum* var. *Nelsonii* A. A.
Eaton]

A few collections have been referred to this hybrid. It closely resembles *E. variegatum* but has deciduous rather than evergreen stems.

CLUB MOSS FAMILY, Lycopodiaceae

Stems creeping, often extensively so, branches upright, leafy; leaves
relatively small, alternate or opposite; sporangia borne in the axils of
leaves, these of the vegetative type or specialized and aggregated in
cones; spores of one kind. (Glossary Plate 4, p. 133)
Represented in Minnesota by a single genus.

Lycopodium L.

Some of the species are rather variable in characters of the branches,
leaves, and cones. Many varieties and forms have been named, but some
of these are certainly no more than individual or ecological variations.
See Victorin, Les Lycopodinées du Quebec, Contrib. Lab. Bot. Univ.
Montréal, No. 3, 1925, for an elaborate treatment of the variations.

KEY TO SPECIES

1. Ultimate branches of the aerial stem roundish; the leaves compara-
   tively large, obvious (as in Fig. 179), not scale-like. 2
   2. Stem creeping, but not extensively so; vegetative branches pros-
      trate or arched, usually rooting at the tip; sporangia borne in a
      sessile cone, the sporangia-bearing leaves quite similar to the vege-
      tative ones . . . . *L. inundatum* (p. 140)
   2. Stem extensively creeping or the branches tufted; vegetative
      branches becoming erect, not rooting at the tip; sporangia borne
      in the axils of leaves similar to the vegetative ones, not in cones,
      or borne in cones and the sporangia-bearing leaves quite different
      from the vegetative ones 3
      3. Main stem at or very near the surface, aerial branches mostly
         erect, sometimes decumbent, branched a few times, the
         secondary branches erect or becoming erect 4

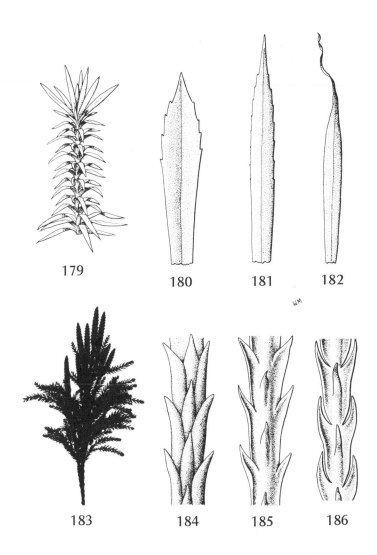

FIGURE 179. *Lycopodium lucidulum*, tip of branch. FIGURE 180. *Lycopodium lucidulum*, leaf. FIGURE 181. *Lycopodium annotinum*, leaf. FIGURE 182. *Lycopodium clavatum*, leaf. FIGURE 183. *Lycopodium obscurum*, stem and branches. FIGURE 184. *Lycopodium complanatum*, portion of branch, upper surface. FIGURE 185. *Lycopodium complanatum*, portion of branch, lower surface. FIGURE 186. *Lycopodium tristachyum*, portion of branch, lower surface.

4. Vegetative and sporangia-bearing leaves with an acute or long-acute tip (Fig. 180), not with a long point; sporangia borne in the axils of leaves similar to the vegetative ones, not in cones 5

   5. Leaves broadest at or near the base, entire or very finely serrate, with stomata on the lower surface and, fewer, on the upper surface . . . . *L. Selago* (p. 137)

   5. Leaves broadest above the middle, usually definitely toothed (especially near the apex), with stomata on the lower surface only (these appearing, under 15X magnification, as small whitish dots). . . . *L. lucidulum* (p. 137)

4. Vegetative leaves with a long, pointed tip (Figs. 181, 182); sporangia borne in cones. 6

   6. Leaves on the aerial branches with a long, straight tip (Fig. 181); cones sessile . . . . . . *L. annotinum* (p. 142)

   6. Leaves on the aerial branches with a very long, more or less twisted tip (Fig. 182); cones stalked . . . .
. . . .*L. clavatum* (p. 143)

3. Main stem deep-seated, aerial branches erect, branched many times, the secondary branches spreading (Fig. 183) 7

   7. Leaves of the lower green portion of the erect stem ascending, the six ranks of leaves of the branchlets arranged in one upper, one lower, and four lateral (two on each side) ranks
. . . . *L. obscurum* (p. 141)

   7. Leaves of the lower green portion of the erect stem divergent, usually widely so, the six ranks of leaves of the branchlets arranged in two upper, two lower, and two lateral (one on each side) ranks . . . .*L. dendroideum* (p. 142)

1. Ultimate branches of the aerial stem flattened or essentially so; leaves scale-like (Fig. 184). 8

   8. Main stem often at or near the surface; leaves on the underside of the ultimate branches of the aerial stem usually poorly developed, usually shorter than the lateral leaves, and distant (Fig. 185); green or glaucous; ultimate branches of the aerial stem relatively broad, mostly about 2 mm. wide, definitely flattened . . . .
. . . .*L. complanatum* (p. 146)

   8. Main stem deep-seated; leaves on the underside of the ultimate branches of the aerial stem well developed, about as long as the lateral leaves and tending to overlap (Fig. 186); heavily glaucous;

ultimate branches of the aerial stem narrow, 1-1.5 mm. wide, not especially flattened . . . . *L. tristachyum* (p. 149)

FIR CLUB-MOSS, *Lycopodium Selago* L., Map 64, Fig. 187

This species and the next, *L. lucidulum*, differ from all of our other species of *Lycopodium* in lacking a cone, the sporangia being borne in the axils of ordinary foliage leaves. Also both frequently bear bulbils (gemmae) in the axils of the upper leaves. *L. Selago* differs from *L. lucidulum* in having entire rather than toothed leaves, and the leaves have stomata on both surfaces rather than on the lower surface only. Also the leaves are all about the same length; in *L. lucidulum* there are definite groups of long leaves alternating with groups of short ones.

It commonly grows on rocks, cliffs, or ledges, sometimes on hillsides, rarely in woods or swamps, in the northeastern part of the state and rarely elsewhere.

Distribution: Greenland to Alaska, south to Alabama, Missouri, Montana, and Washington; Eurasia.

SHINING CLUB-MOSS, *Lycopodium lucidulum* Michx., Map 65, Fig. 188

The Shining Club-moss rather closely resembles the Fir Club-moss, and most of the differences are discussed under that species. In addi-

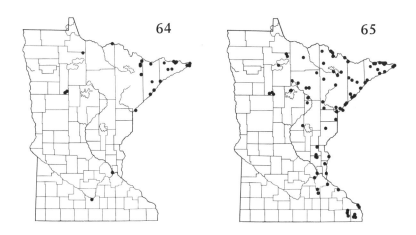

MAP 64. *Lycopodium Selago.*   MAP 65. *Lycopodium lucidulum.*

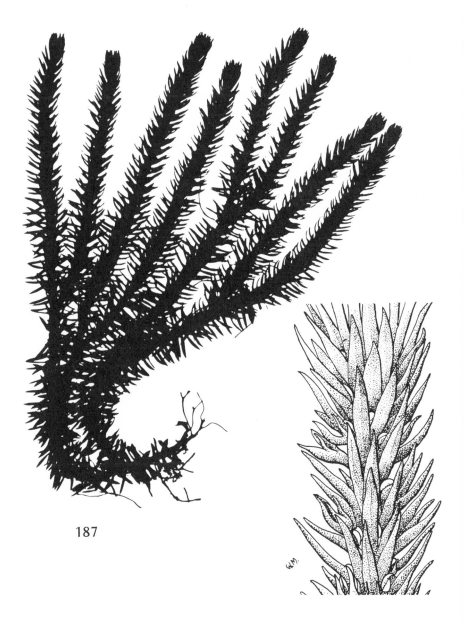

187

FIGURE 187. *Lycopodium Selago*, lower right, portion of fertile stem (enlarged); upper left, fertile plant 15 cm. tall.

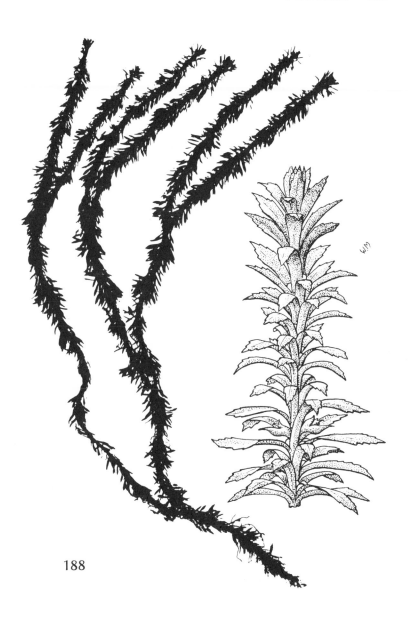

188

FIGURE 188. *Lycopodium lucidulum: left,* fertile plant 40 cm. tall; *right,* tip of fertile stem (enlarged).

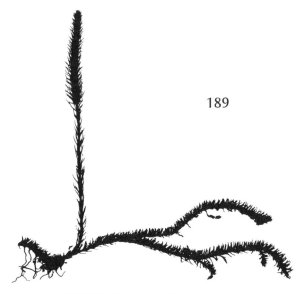

189

FIGURE 189. *Lycopodium inundatum*,
fertile plant 10 cm. tall.

tion the Shining Club-moss has the leaves broadest above the middle, lanceolate-obovate, rather than broadest at the base. Like *L. Selago* it frequently has bulbils in the axils of the upper leaves. A phase with the leaves entire or nearly so is represented by a few specimens from Minnesota. It intergrades imperceptibly with the form with toothed leaves.

This species grows in moist woods and swamps, on hillsides, and occasionally on cliffs and ledges, in the eastern half of the state.

Distribution: Newfoundland to Minnesota, south to South Carolina and Missouri.

BOG CLUB-MOSS, *Lycopodium inundatum* L., Map 66, Fig. 189

This is our smallest species and also the only one that characteristically grows in open, moist places. The leaves are rather thin and frequently have a few large teeth. The sporangia are borne in a cone, but the leaves of the cone are quite similar to the vegetative ones.

It grows in moss, peat, or sandy soil in meadows, on lake shores or other open, moist or wet places, in the east-central part of the state.

Distribution: Newfoundland to Alaska, south to Virginia, Idaho, and Oregon: Eurasia.

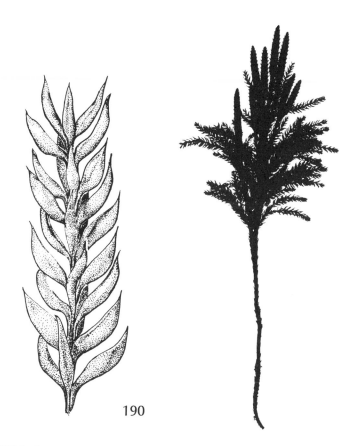

190

FIGURE 190. *Lycopodium obscurum* var. *isophyllum: right,* fertile stem
25 cm. tall; *left,* portion of branchlet, view of upper side (enlarged).

GROUND-PINE, *Lycopodium obscurum* L., Map 67, Fig. 190

This species and the next are distinctive in having an erect stem
branched in a bushy manner. The main stem is creeping rather deep in
the soil and is not obtained in most collections.

The distinctive characters of *L. obscurum* are the ascending leaves of
the main erect stem and the leaves of the branchlets that are arranged in
one upper, one lower, and two lateral ranks on each side. In Minnesota
is var. *isophyllum* Hickey, all the leaves of which are nearly the same
length.

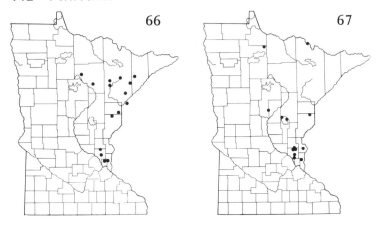

MAP 66. *Lycopodium inundatum*. MAP 67. *Lycopodium obscurum* var. *isophyllum*

It grows in woods and meadows, rarely on rocks, in several of the eastern and northern counties.

Distribution: Variety *isophyllum* ranges from Newfoundland to North Carolina, west to Minnesota; var. *obscurum*, with leaves of the lower rank shorter, is in Michigan and eastward.

ROUND-BRANCHED GROUND-PINE, *Lycopodium dendroideum* Michx. [*Lycopodium obscurum* L. var. *dendroideum* (Michx.) D. C. Eaton] Map 68, Fig. 191

This species resembles the previous one, but is clearly separated from it by the spreading leaves of the main erect stem and the arrangement of the leaves on the branchlets. These leaves are in two upper and two lower ranks and one lateral rank on each side.

It grows in hardwoods, in coniferous woods, and in thickets, often in sandy soil and rarely in rocky places. It is common in the northeast but rare and local to the south.

Distribution: Labrador to North Carolina, west to Washington and Alaska; eastern Asia.

BRISTLY CLUB-MOSS, *Lycopodium annotinum* L., Map 69, Fig. 192

The aerial branches have the general aspect of *L. lucidulum*, but fertile specimens can be easily separated by the sessile cone and sterile ones by the pointed leaves.

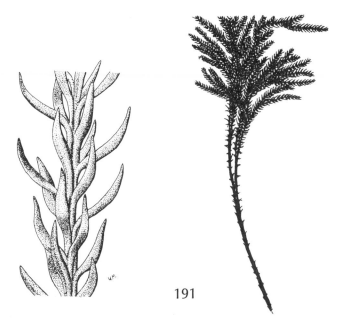

191

FIGURE 191. *Lycopodium dendroideum: right*, fertile stem, portion 20 cm. tall; *left*, portion of branchlet, view of upper side (enlarged).

The species shows considerable differences in the toothing and orientation of the leaves. Although these variations are sometimes considered to be varieties, it is more likely that they are ecological forms, without taxonomic importance.

Typical *L. annotinum* is illustrated in Fig. 192B, var. *acrifolium* Fernald in Fig. 192C, and var. *pungens* (La Pylaie) Desv. in Fig. 192D.

Lycopodium annotinum grows in woods, on higher sites in wooded swamps, and in rocky places.

Distribution: Greenland to Alaska, south to Virginia, Colorado and Oregon; Eurasia.

RUNNING CLUB-MOSS, *Lycopodium clavatum* L., Map 70, Fig. 193

The long, weak points on the leaves distinguish this species from the others. The stem is very long, usually creeping on top of the ground.

Several variations have been recognized based on the lengths of the peduncles, pedicels, and cones, the number of cones and appressed or

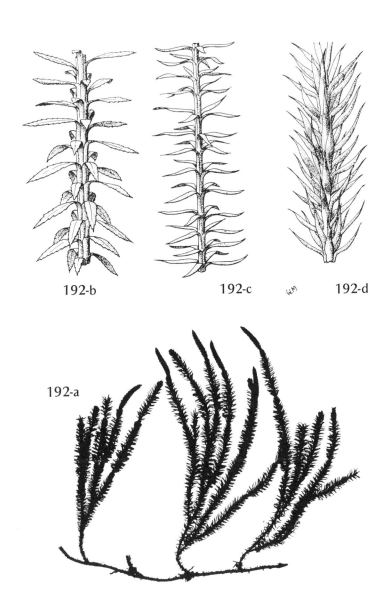

192-b   192-c   (WM)   192-d

192-a

FIGURE 192. *Lycopodium annotinum*: 192A, fertile plant 20 cm. tall; 192B, portion of stem (enlarged); 192C, portion of stem (enlarged); 192D, portion of stem (enlarged).

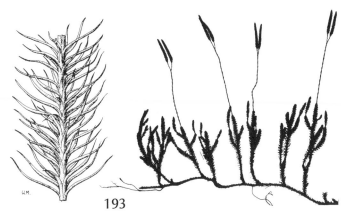

FIGURE 193. *Lycopodium clavatum: left,* portion of stem (enlarged), *right,* fertile plant 25 cm. tall.

spreading leaves. None of these variations are at all well marked in Minnesota, the essential characters varying even on the same plant.

The Running Club-moss grows in thickets, coniferous woods, and mixed woods, and sometimes on swamp borders, in deciduous woods, or in rocky places. It is most common in St. Louis, Lake, and Cook counties, infrequent in a few counties westward and southward.

Distribution: Newfoundland to Alaska, south to North Carolina, Minnesota, and Oregon; Eurasia.

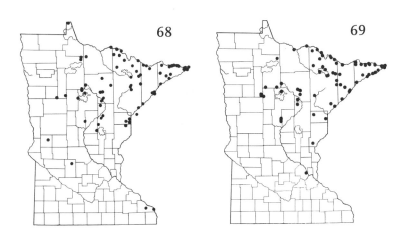

MAP 68. *Lycopodium dendroideum.* MAP 69. *Lycopodium annotinum.*

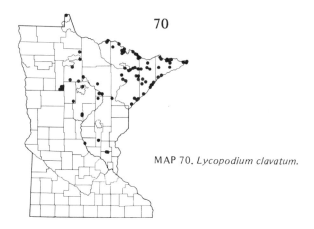

MAP 70. *Lycopodium clavatum.*

GROUND CEDAR, *Lycopodium complanatum* L.

This species and the next, *L. tristachyum*, are distinctive among our Lycopodiums in having scale-like leaves and rather flattened branches. The differences are discussed under *L. tristachyum* where it is mentioned that the two intergrade in a number of characters. The two varieties of *L. complanatum* also intergrade with each other. Intermediates are sometimes recognized as hybrids, but the variation in this complex is not well understood and it may have a strong ecological basis.

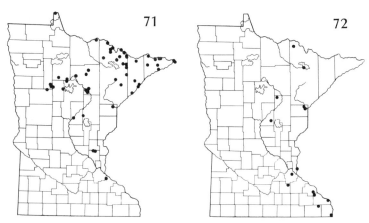

MAP 71. *Lycopodium complanatum* var. *complanatum*. MAP 72. *Lycopodium complanatum* var. *flabelliforme.*

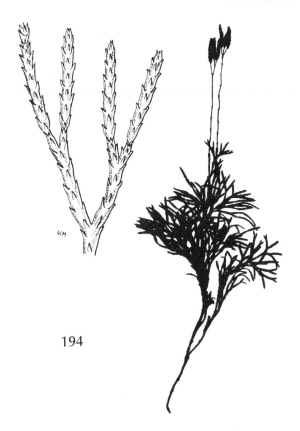

194

FIGURE 194. *Lycopodium complanatum* var. *complanatum: upper left,* portion of branches, lower surface (enlarged); *right,* fertile stem 25 cm. tall.

L. complanatum var. *complanatum*, Map 71, Fig. 194

The branches are rather irregularly disposed, not definitely fan-like; there are evident constrictions on many of the branches marking the end of each year's growth, and the leaves on the under surface of the branch are poorly developed.

Victorin has described two variations that belong here (var. *canadense* and var. *elongatum*) based on characters of the main stem, length of the aerial branches and peduncles, and number of cones and cones sessile or pedicellate. The characters concerned are all quite variable and different numbers of cones and sessile or pedicellate cones occur on the

FIGURE 195. *Lycopodium complanatum* var. *flabelliforme:*
right, portion of branches, lower surface (enlarged);
upper left and *lower*, fertile stems 30 cm. tall.

same plant, the same year, or in different years. The typical variety
grows in coniferous woods, ravines, or rocky places in the north-central
and northeastern parts of the state.

Distribution: Newfoundland to Alaska, south to Pennsylvania, Montana, and Washington; Eurasia.

L. complanatum var. *flabelliforme* Fernald, Map 72, Fig. 195

This variety has the branches spreading in a fan-like manner and
lacks the constrictions characteristic of var. *complanatum*.

It has been collected in a pine forest and on a wooded hillside in the southeastern part of the state and, occasionally, northward.

Distribution: Newfoundland to Minnesota, south to Georgia and Iowa.

GROUND CEDAR, *Lycopodium tristachyum* Pursh, Map 73, Fig. 196

This species is characterized by a deep-seated main stem, very glaucous branches, and rather well developed leaves on the lower side of the branches. It is usually treated as a distinct species but actually intergrades with *L. complanatum* in all characters and, at least in Minnesota, seems to be a well marked extreme of that species.

It grows in coniferous woods and on rocks in the northeastern one-third of the state.

Distribution: New Brunswick to Minnesota, south to Alabama.

HYBRID

Lycopodium lucidulum X *Lycopodium Selago* [*Lycopodium* X *Buttersii* Abbe]

This proposed hybrid is intermediate between *L. lucidulum* and *L. Selago*. It has some leaves with stomata on the upper surface, as in *L. Selago*; the leaves are mostly toothed but not as strongly as in *L. lucidulum*, and some on a branch are entire; there is a strongly developed tendency toward alternate sets of short and long leaves, but this is not as pronounced as in *L. lucidulum*.

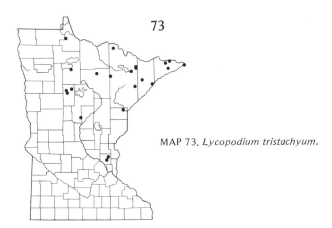

73

MAP 73. *Lycopodium tristachyum.*

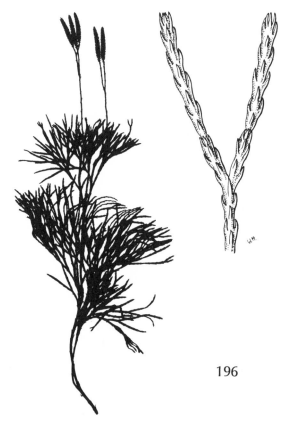

196

FIGURE 196. *Lycopodium tristachyum: left,* fertile stem 25 cm. tall;
right, portion of branches, lower surface (enlarged).

It has been collected in Lake and Cook counties.
Distribution: Minnesota.

SPIKE MOSS FAMILY, Selaginellaceae

Stems creeping, branches upright or ascending, leafy; leaves relatively small, alternate; sporangia borne in the axils of specialized leaves aggregated into cones; spores of two kinds borne in separate sporangia.
Represented in Minnesota by a single genus.

197

FIGURE 197. *Selaginella selaginoides: upper left*, fertile
tip of stem (enlarged); *upper right*, sterile portion of stem
(enlarged); *lower*, fertile plants, the right one 3 cm. tall.

Selaginella Beauv.

MOUNTAIN MOSS, *Selaginella selaginoides* (L.) Link, Map 74, Fig. 197

The thin leaves with toothed margins separate this species from the
next. It is a small species and does not grow in large mats as *S. rupestris*
often does.

It has been collected in mossy places on Long Island and Big Susie
Island near Grand Portage and at Grand Marais.

Distribution: Greenland to Alaska, south to Maine, Michigan, Colorado, and British Columbia.

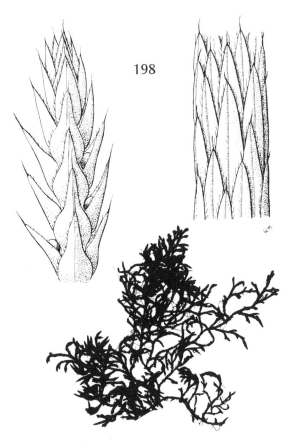

FIGURE 198. *Selaginella rupestris: upper left*, fertile
tip of stem (enlarged); *upper right*, sterile portion of
stem (enlarged); *lower*, fertile plant,
the mat 9 cm. across.

ROCK SPIKE-MOSS, *Selaginella rupestris* (L.) Spring, Map 75, Fig. 198

This species usually grows in mats; its thick leaves with ciliate margins separate it from the previous species.

It grows throughout the state, most commonly on exposed acidic rocks, sometimes on other types of rocks or in sand.

Distribution: Greenland to Alberta, south to Georgia and Oklahoma.

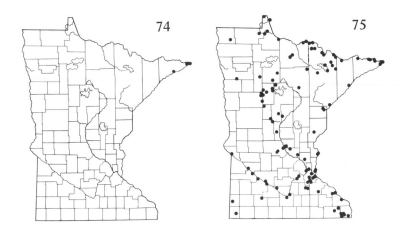

MAP 74. *Selaginella selaginoides.* MAP 75. *Selaginella rupestris.*

QUILLWORT FAMILY, Isoëtaceae

Stem corm-like, short and erect, bearing awl-shaped, alternate leaves from the terminal portion and roots from the basal; leaves expanded at the base, the fertile ones with a large sporangium on the inner face; spores of two kinds borne in separate sporangia.

Represented in Minnesota by a single genus.

Isoëtes L.

The species of this genus can be critically identified only by the megaspores that are borne in the sporangia at the bases of the leaves. *I. echinospora* var. *Braunii* has a spiny megaspore; the other two species have ridged ones. The megaspores of *I. melanopoda* are about half the size (averaging 0.35 mm. in diameter) of those of *I. macrospora* (averaging 0.7 mm.).

PRAIRIE QUILLWORT, *Isoëtes melanopoda* Gay & Durieu, Map 76, Fig. 199

The leaves of this species are usually longer than those of our other two species, and it often grows in wet mud or only partly submerged rather than completely submerged. The megaspores are slightly ridged, not spiny, and are about half as large as those of *I. macrospora* (aver-

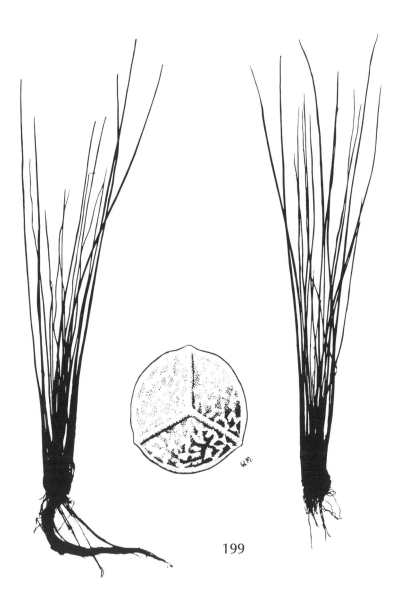

FIGURE 199. *Isoëtes melanopoda: left* and *right*, plants 20 cm.
tall; *center*, megaspore (magnified).

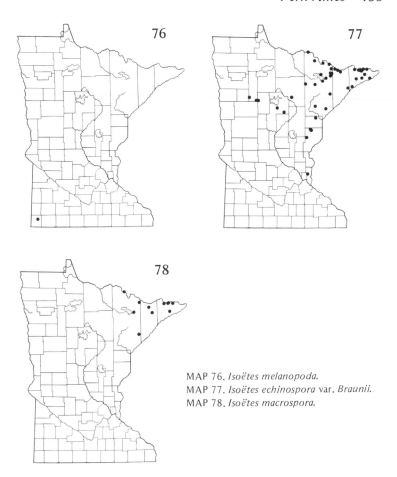

MAP 76. *Isoëtes melanopoda.*
MAP 77. *Isoëtes echinospora* var. *Braunii.*
MAP 78. *Isoëtes macrospora.*

aging 0.35 mm. in diameter). The bases of the leaves are usually either black or dark brown and shining.

It has been collected once in prairie pools in the southwestern corner of the state.

Distribution: Illinois to Minnesota, south to Texas.

BRAUN'S QUILLWORT, *Isoëtes echinospora* Dur. var. *Braunii* (Dur.) Engelm., Map 77, Fig. 200 [*Isoëtes muricata* Dur.; *Isoëtes Braunii* Dur.]

This species bears spiny megaspores about 0.5 mm. in diameter. It grows in lakes or rivers, usually submerged but sometimes barely

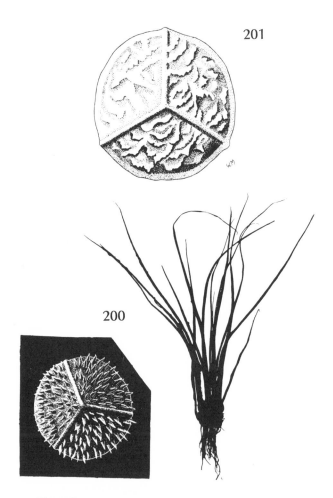

FIGURE 200. *Isoëtes echinospora* var. *Braunii: left*, megaspore (magnified); *right*, plant 10 cm. tall. FIGURE 201. *Isoëtes macrospora*, megaspore (magnified).

emergent, the submerged plants mostly growing at a depth of about one foot but sometimes at a depth of up to three or five feet of water. It is most common in the northeastern part of the state.

Distribution: Newfoundland to Minnesota, south to Pennsylvania and Ohio; other varieties occur in the eastern and western United States, Canada, and Europe.

LAKE QUILLWORT, *Isoëtes macrospora* Durieu, Map 78, Fig. 201

The general habit of this species is similar to that of Braun's Quillwort (Fig. 200). The ridged rather than spiny megaspores distinguish it, however, as does the size of the megaspores, which are about 0.7 mm. in diameter.

It grows submerged in lakes in St. Louis, Cook, and Lake counties.

Distribution: Newfoundland to New Jersey, west to Minnesota.

INDEX

Index

The page numbers in bold face indicate the primary text reference.

161